THE
LAUGH
OUT
LOUD
GUIDE

Ace the SAT* Exam without

Boring Yourself to Sleep!

THE LAUGH OUT LOUD GUIDE

Ace the SAT* Exam without

Boring Yourself to Sleep!

Charles Horn, PhD

**Andrews McMeel
Publishing, LLC**

Kansas City

08 09 10 11 12 WKT 10 9 8 7 6 5 4 3 2 1

ISBN-13: 978-0-7407-7710-3
ISBN-10: 0-7407-7710-6

Library of Congress Control Number: 2008922541

Illustrations on pages 73, 107, 109, 160, and 163 courtesy
of Marc Stoksik

*ŚAT is a registered trademark of the College Board, which was
not involved in the production of, and does not endorse, this
product.

www.andrewsmcmeel.com

ATTENTION: SCHOOLS AND BUSINESSES
Andrews McMeel books are available at quantity discounts
with bulk purchase for educational, business, or sales promotional
use. For information, please write to: Special Sales Department,
Andrews McMeel Publishing, LLC, 1130 Walnut Street,
Kansas City, Missouri 64106.

CONTENTS

PART 7: ANSWERS

PREFACE

Every year, almost two million students like yourself take the SAT* exam, a test that will affect your college admission, scholarship offers, future career, what car you'll drive, how much money you'll make, and basically the rest of your entire life. No pressure, right?

The problem with most SAT* study guides is they're written as textbooks—tedious, not relatable, and politically correct. When you try to study from these guides, you feel like you're in another boring class at school until finally you just plain fall asleep.

The Laugh Out Loud Guide was written specifically to engage, take the pressure off, and help you learn the material as you laugh your way to a higher test score. The focus is on working through sample questions that are funny and relatable, and thus engaging and much more memorable. You'll learn everything you need to know in order to ace the SAT* exam, remember it all when you need it on test day, and you may even have a little fun along the way!

ACKNOWLEDGMENTS

I would like to thank a number of people for their contributions to the making of this book. Thank you to my literary agent, Julie May, for her efforts in selling the project, and for really "getting" the idea right from the start. Thank you to my editor, Lane Butler, and all the fine folks at Andrews McMeel for the really amazing work they've done putting it all together. Thank you to Marc Stoksik for providing his wonderful, funny drawings. Thanks to everyone who proofed or gave notes on various drafts or portions, including Judy Brown, David Isaac, Steven Eli Posner, Carla Robinson, and Janet Elise. Finally, special thanks again to Janet, who also helped put me in touch with Julie, and generally championed the book (and me) throughout.

PART 1

SO YOU'RE GOING TO TAKE THE SAT* EXAM . . .

So You're Going to Take the SAT* Exam…

When you hear the words SAT* exam do you start to sweat? If someone says it do you immediately begin quaking in fear? Then you may be suffering from SAT-itis. Well, lucky for you, we've got the cure. Side effects may include increasing your test score, getting into the Ivy League school of your choice, scholarship offers, and the life of your dreams.

THE LAUGH OUT LOUD GUIDE APPROACH

Okay, so you looked at a sample SAT* exam or tried to read another SAT* study guide, fell asleep a couple of times, and now you think you're stupid. Sorry to break it to you, but maybe you're just bored. Let's try learning this stuff again, only now with fun questions.

Let's face it—the SAT* exam is BORING and OUT OF TOUCH! Who the heck cares about their stupid questions? They make this test so freaking important to your future and then they go out of their way to make it the most mind-numbing snorefest possible. That hardly seems fair, but what can you do?

The idea behind *The Laugh Out Loud Guide* is to teach you everything you need to know about the exam, but with questions that are funny and topics you can relate to. Topics include pop culture, Hollywood, sports, sex, drugs, and rock 'n' roll—in other words, things people actually talk about, rather than stuffy, politically correct, and *BORING* textbook material.

The material in this book is totally educational and accurate, but why should that stop us from being engaging and laugh-out-loud funny at the same time?

THE COMEDY EDGE™

Too often in school, you're led to believe that the learning process must be dull and dry. You're taught that anything funny and outrageous can't be educational as well.

However, just the opposite is true. Research shows that comedy enhances learning, reduces stress (which makes it easier to absorb material), makes subjects more interesting (so you'll want to learn them in the first place), and increases recall (so you'll remember the material better on test day).

Common sense tells you this as well. How long do you remember most facts you learn in school? A day? A week? Two weeks? On the other hand, how long do you remember lines from your favorite TV show or movie?

Comedy can, in fact, be the edge you need to get ahead. So if anyone questions how much you'll learn from a comedic study guide, simply remember the following: While some of your unlucky friends will be forced to study for the SAT* exam in their knickers and granny panties—the same old boring way their parents and grandparents did before them—you'll be laughing your way to a higher test score, enjoying the full advantage of The Comedy Edge™.

STRUCTURE OF THIS BOOK

This book has two main components: review and practice questions. The review chapters (parts 2–5) describe, with examples, each of the three portions of the SAT*exam and all the types of questions you'll find on the exam. We'll also tell you exactly how to approach each type of question, with a focus on actual concrete examples.

The second component of the book (parts 6 and 7) consists of sections of practice questions and answers. Each practice section is organized exactly like an actual section of the test, so you can practice the material and get used to the structure of the test at the same time.

HOW TO USE THIS BOOK

Um, may we suggest . . . reading it?

Seriously, read this book and work through the practice sections. You can either flip back and forth between the review and practice sections, or you can complete the entire review first and then move on to the practice sections. It's totally up to you. Then, once you've completed this book and have a firm grasp of the material, go out and get some official SAT* practice tests. Take a practice test and amaze yourself at how much you've learned.

That's about it. The next chapter contains answers to some frequently asked questions on the basics of the SAT* exam, which many of you may know already. If you're already familiar with the basics, feel free to skim through the next chapter or jump to the following one.

Let the fun begin!

SAT* Exam FAQ

Q. DO I REALLY HAVE TO TAKE THIS TEST?

A. If you want to get accepted into a college or university that requires SAT* exam scores (and most of them do), yes. If you want to work at McDonalds, probably not.

Q. HOW LONG IS THE TEST?

A. It's 3 hours and 45 minutes (not including breaks). It only *feels like* forever.

Q. WHAT DO I NEED TO BRING WITH ME TO THE TEST?

A. Your admission ticket, a photo ID, some No. 2 pencils, an eraser, and a calculator. You should also bring a watch if you want to keep track of your time during the test. Clothing is *NOT* optional.

Q. DO I NEED TO PROVIDE A URINE SAMPLE?

A. No. Steroid away!

Q. WHAT'S ON THE TEST?

A. There are three parts: Critical Reading, Writing, and Math. A detailed breakdown for each part can be found in the review chapters of this book.

Q. IS IT ALL MULTIPLE CHOICE?

A. Most of it is, but there's also a written essay and 10 grid-in questions, which are math questions that aren't multiple choice.

Q. SHOULD I GUESS IF I DON'T KNOW THE ANSWER TO A QUESTION?

A. It depends how lucky you feel. For multiple-choice questions, you're penalized a quarter of a point for each question that you answer and get wrong. Statistically speaking, it's okay to guess, and even advisable to guess if you can eliminate at least one of the answer choices. For the grid-in questions, you don't get penalized for wrong answers, so always guess on grid-ins even if you have no clue what the answer is.

Q. CAN I CHEAT?

A. You can try, but if you get caught you'll be expelled from the test. You'll also be arrested by the SAT* police, and those nerds are just itching for trouble!

Q. HOW ARE THESE THINGS SCORED?

A. For each of the Critical Reading, Writing, and Math portions, they'll add up all the questions you got right and subtract any penalties for wrong answers. They'll also add in the score for your essay to your overall score on the Writing portion. After they've done all that, they'll convert these three raw scores to three scaled scores between 200 and 800. A score of 800 in all three portions—otherwise known as a perfect 2400—means you're probably getting into any school you want (and you're a virgin). A score of 200 in all three portions—otherwise known as the 600 of shame—means you should probably start memorizing the phrase, "Would you like fries with that?" Together with the 200–800 scores, they'll also give you percentiles, which tell you how well you did relative to everyone else taking the test.

Q. CAN I USE A CALCULATOR FOR THE MATH SECTIONS?

A. No, only for the English sections. Duh! Yes, you can bring a simple calculator, a scientific calculator, or even a graphing calculator, but not a computer. Your calculator can't have a typewriter-style keypad, can't print, can't make noise, and shouldn't require an electrical outlet. Remember to bring your own calculator, because you won't be provided with one, and also make sure the batteries are fresh. It might also be a good idea to actually know how to use the calculator beforehand instead of trying to figure it out during the test.

Q. CAN I PAY SOMEONE TO TAKE THE TEST FOR ME?

A. It's possible, but you'll either need to get them a primo fake ID or agree to undergo plastic surgery. Your photo ID in the hands of a brilliant Asian kid probably won't cut it.

Q. CAN I AT LEAST SIT NEXT TO SOME ASIAN KIDS SO I CAN COPY THEIR ANSWERS?

A. Wow, you have a real fascination with Asian kids, don't you? Hasn't anyone ever taught you that stereotypes are bad? Anyway, everyone around you will be given a test with the sections arranged in a different order than yours, so no dice. Nice try, though.

Q. CAN I BRING SOMETHING TO EAT?

A. Yes, but you're not allowed to eat while taking the test. You can eat during breaks. Try to avoid ingesting sleeping pills before or during the test.

Q. HOW OFTEN IS THE TEST OFFERED?

A. Seven times a year in the United States and six times a year outside of the United States. U-S-A! U-S-A!

Q. WHAT IF I GET ALL THE ANSWERS RIGHT BUT MY DOG EATS MY ANSWER SHEETS?

A. Your dog isn't even supposed to be in the exam room, so you're probably on pretty thin ice with that one.

Q. CAN I TAKE THE TEST MORE THAN ONCE?

A. Yes, you SAT*-lover, you.

Q. IF I'M SMART AND DID WELL IN ALL MY CLASSES, WHY DO I NEED A STUDY GUIDE?

A. The SAT* exam doesn't just test what you learned in school—it's a reasoning test as well. There are specific question types, specific approaches, and specific pitfalls you should learn about. Plus, the difference of a few percentiles at the top end can mean the difference between Ivy League and state school, and between full scholarships and massive debt for the next decade or so. Anyway, do you ever really need a reason to study?

Q. BUT I'M AFRAID OF TESTS.

A. I'm sorry, can you please rephrase that in the form of a question?

Q. WHAT DO I DO IF I'M AFRAID OF TESTS?

A. Tests are only scary when you're not prepared for them, and you won't ever become prepared if you're bored to sleep by the other books out there. On the other hand, by the time you finish *this* book, you'll be too busy laughing to be afraid of anything. Plus, you'll have a much better time remembering everything on the day of the test.

Q. BUT I'M A JOCK AND I'M JUST NOT GOOD AT THIS STUFF.

A. <cough, cough>

Q. FINE. IF I'M A JOCK, WHY SHOULD I TAKE THIS TEST?

A. Thank you! Not everyone needs to score a perfect 2400 to get into college. You probably know a lot more than you think you do and you most likely only need to achieve some minimum score anyway to receive your athletic scholarship. Then it's a life of frat parties and Spring Break! Reading this book suddenly seems like a very small price to pay, don't you think?

Q. HOW DO I STUDY FOR THE SAT* EXAM?

A. Try this simple three-step formula for success:
1. Buy this book!
2. Read this book!
3. Work through official SAT* tests. You might be able to obtain official practice tests through your school, or you can buy *The Official SAT Study Guide*, from College Board, the makers of the SAT* exam.

   When you're happy with your score on the official practice tests, that's when you know you're ready.

Q. SHOULD I TAKE AN SAT* CLASS?

A. If you take the time to read this book and work through official sample practice tests, you shouldn't need to take a class. However, if you find that you're just not getting anywhere on your own, need the classroom structure in order to learn, and can afford the expense, go for it. Some people say classes really helped them, while others say they were useless and a huge rip-off. Spend a little time with this book first before blowing tons of money on a class. Unless, of course, the class uses this book as a text, in which case, you should absolutely take it. And tell all your friends! ☺

Q. SHOULD I GET A TUTOR?

A. Again, this book together with sample tests should be sufficient, but if you really work best one-on-one with a tutor, go for it. If you're rich there are numerous tutoring companies happy to take your (or your parent's) money. If you're poor and want a tutor, see what resources your school has, or even try Craigslist. While many tutoring companies charge over $100 an hour, what they probably won't tell you is that they only pay many of their tutors $20–$30 an hour and pocket the rest. As you can imagine, the tutors are probably not very happy about that and these are the people you're depending on to teach you. Independent tutors can be a better deal for everyone involved as they cut out the middleman and also won't lock you into long-term, high-priced commitments. Of course, if a tutoring company uses this book as their text then they must truly be a wonderful company and are worth every penny. ☺

Q. WHERE CAN I GO FOR THE MOST UP-TO-DATE INFORMATION?

A. The College Board Web site (*www.collegeboard.com*) is the place to go for the most up-to-date info on the test. You can find upcoming test dates, locations, and prices, as well as tons of other useful (and useless) information.

PART 2
CRITICAL READING

Critical Reading Overview

The Critical Reading portion of the SAT* exam consists of two types of questions:

- *Sentence completions*

- *Critical reading passages*

Sentence completions take less time, so you should do them first. Most questions, though, involve the critical reading passages, and take much longer to complete.

The typical breakdown of the Critical Reading portion looks something like this:

CRITICAL READING: 3 SECTIONS	
TYPE OF QUESTIONS	**NO. OF QUESTIONS**
Sentence completions	19 questions
Critical reading passages	48 questions

TYPICAL SECTION BREAKDOWNS*

25-MINUTE SECTION	24 QUESTIONS
5 sentence completions	5 questions
2 short passages	4 questions
1 medium-length passage	6 questions
1 long passage	9 questions

25-MINUTE SECTION	24 QUESTIONS
8 sentence completions	8 questions
1 medium-length passage	4 questions
1 long passage	12 questions

20-MINUTE SECTION	19 QUESTIONS
6 sentence completions	6 questions
1 really long passage	13 questions

*The section breakdowns vary slightly from test to test, but this is a good indication of what to expect.

Sentence Completions

For sentence completions, you're given a sentence with missing words and you have to fill in the blanks from one of the five answer choices. Some sentences have one missing word, while others have two.

For example:

1. Yo Momma so _____, when you mail her a letter, you need two zip codes.
   (A) diaphanous
   (B) luminous
   (C) ravenous
   (D) grisly
   (E) corpulent

2. The cannibals thought that, while Diego was tough and _____, Dora the Explorer was absolutely _____.
   (A) stringy, bland
   (B) unsavory, delectable
   (C) succulent, piquant
   (D) luscious, insipid
   (E) delicious, appetizing

Sentence completions test your vocabulary knowledge and your reasoning skills to determine which word or words *best* fill in the blanks in the context of each of the sentences. Some sentences contain harder words than others.

HOW TO SOLVE SENTENCE COMPLETIONS

Let's examine the previous two examples and see how we can work through each of them.

---

1. Yo Momma so _____, when you mail her a letter, you need two zip codes.
    (A) diaphanous
    (B) luminous
    (C) ravenous
    (D) grisly
    (E) corpulent

ANSWER: **E**

SOLUTION: If I need to use two zip codes rather than one in order to mail a letter to your mother, then your mother must take up a whole lot of physical space—in other words she must be pretty darn fat. So the missing word must mean *huge* or *fat*.

This is a difficult question because the answer choices contain difficult words. Let's take a look at each of the answer choices:

    A. *Diaphanous* means *transparent* or *see-through*, so that doesn't fit.

    B. *Luminous* means *glowing* or *shining*, so that doesn't fit.

    C. *Ravenous* means *extremely hungry*, so that doesn't quite fit. Your mother is so fat she may always be hungry too, but *hungry* isn't the word we're looking for here.

    D. *Grisly* means *gruesome* or *horrible*, so that doesn't fit (although I'm guessing your mother is probably pretty gruesome-looking as well).

    E. *Corpulent* means *extremely fat*, which is the word we were looking for here.

THE CORRECT ANSWER IS (E).

---

2. The cannibals thought that, while Diego was tough and _____, Dora the Explorer was absolutely _____.
    (A) stringy, bland
    (B) unsavory, delectable
    (C) succulent, piquant
    (D) luscious, insipid
    (E) delicious, appetizing

ANSWER: **B**

SOLUTION: Two key words in the sentence help us a lot here. The word *while* tells us that the two blanks should be somewhat opposite to each other. In other words, while Diego was *one thing*, Dora the Explorer was *something very different and opposite*. In addition, the word *and* in "tough and _____" tells us that just like the word *tough* is meant negatively, so too should the first blank mean something negative.

    With all of that in mind, let's take a look at the answer choices:

A. *Tough* and *stringy* fit together, but *stringy* and *bland* are both negative words, so this isn't the right answer.

B. *Tough* and *unsavory* fit together, and *unsavory* and *delectable* are opposites, so this looks like a good match.

C. *Tough* and *succulent* don't fit together. This isn't the right answer. (*Piquant* means spicy, by the way. Being a Latina, Dora is probably spicy, but *succulent* doesn't fit into the first blank so we have to eliminate this answer choice.)

D. *Tough* and *luscious* don't fit together. This isn't the right answer. (*Insipid* means *dull*, by the way.)

E. *Tough* and *delicious* don't fit together. This isn't the right answer.

THE CORRECT ANSWER IS (B).

General Approach for Sentences with One Blank

- Read the entire sentence first to get an overall sense of understanding.

- Look at each answer choice and for each one see if the sentence makes sense with that word. If the sentence doesn't make sense with that word, cross off that choice as incorrect.

- If the sentence makes sense with that word, that choice may be the correct answer, *BUT DO NOT STOP THERE*. You should (at least briefly) examine all of the answer choices, because one of the other choices may be an even better fit to the sentence.

- Once you've made your choice, double-check your answer by quickly re-reading the entire sentence with the missing word filled in.

- If you have no clue about the meaning of some of the words, cross off as many answers as you can, and depending on how many choices are left, decide if you want to guess.

Speeding Up the Process

    When you first read the sentence, a word may already come to your mind before even looking at the answer choices. If you think of a word, quickly look through the answer choices to find either the word you thought of, or a word that means the same thing.

    Remember to look at each answer choice, though, in case two of the choices have similar meanings. In our first example, only one word meant *fat*, so we knew right away—assuming we knew what *corpulent* meant—that was the right answer. Suppose, however, we were given another choice that also meant *fat*. Suppose the question was:

3. Yo Momma so _____, when you mail her a letter, you need two zip codes.
   (A) diaphanous
   (B) chubby
   (C) ravenous
   (D) grisly
   (E) corpulent

The word *chubby* also means *fat*, so what do we do? Well, we consider the overall meaning of the sentence to see that your mother isn't just *fat*, but *extremely fat*, so we should choose whichever answer better conveys the notion of *extremely fat*. *Chubby* doesn't quite convey just how fat your mother really is, so the better choice is still *corpulent*.

General Approach for Sentences with Two Blanks

- Focus on one blank at a time and apply the same techniques you just learned for the one-blank questions.

- Remember, both words in the answer have to make sense within the sentence. So, if the first word in the answer choice doesn't make sense in the first blank, then you can immediately cross off that choice. Similarly, if the second word in the answer choice doesn't make sense in the second blank, you can immediately cross off that choice. Because there are two chances of eliminating each answer choice, two-blank questions can sometimes be even easier to answer correctly than one-blank questions.

- Pay very close attention to words in the sentence that relate the two blanks together. Words like *while, but, and, although, however,* and *yet* can let you know how different parts of the sentence are either comparable or contrasting.

WAYS TO IMPROVE YOUR SCORE

1. Increase Your Vocabulary

Increasing your vocabulary is probably the most important way to help you achieve a higher score. Obviously, someone who knows the meaning of the word "corpulent" in our first example has a much better shot at getting that question right.

So how do you increase your vocabulary? Some people swear by Word-a-Day calendars, some people do crossword puzzles, some people use flash cards or other vocabulary builders, and some wackos even try to memorize the dictionary. There's really no substitute for reading, though. Pick up a decent novel, or a book on your favorite subject, and whenever you come across a word you don't understand, look it up in the dictionary. You'll remember the words a lot better if you remember where you read them, rather than if you just blindly try to memorize words from the dictionary or vocabulary lists.

By the way, just because you're able to increase your vocabulary and learn a bunch of big, new, fancy words, that doesn't mean you'll be forced to use them in everyday life. You can still choose to act dumb around that stud quarterback or hot cheerleader in order not to scare them away. Don't worry; we won't tell.

2. Practice

Practice the techniques you learned in this section. Pay attention to key words in the sentence that tell you how each blank relates to the rest of the sentence or to another blank.

Critical Reading Passages

The majority of the Critical Reading sections on the SAT* exam consist of critical reading passages. In a nutshell, you're given passages to read and you have to answer questions about them.

Some passages are short, consisting of a single paragraph, while other passages are big-ass long. Some passages are made up of two smaller passages put together, both related to each other. The longer the passage, the more questions you'll have to answer on that passage.

For example:

Questions 1–5 are based on the following passage.

Microsoft, the world's largest software maker, warned consumers today about a critical flaw in their Windows operating system, the operating system used in the computers of virtually every business and person on the planet not smart
Line enough to buy a Mac.
5 Today's critical flaw actually follows yet another critical flaw last week, three "quite serious" flaws two weeks ago, one "super-duper" flaw last month, and of course last year's "D'oh!" Today's flaw was in fact serious enough for Bill Gates to raise the Hacker Threat Level to Orange.
Experts warn that, until a software patch is installed, a malicious hacker
10 could use the flaw to take control of your computer, delete your data, eavesdrop on sensitive information, and even steal the porn straight off your hard drive.
To fix the flaw is simple. Just open up your Internet browser, go to the Microsoft Web site, left-click under Resources slash Windows Update, then left-click on Install Latest Windows Update Software, left-click on Scan For
15 Updates, review Critical Updates, left-click Download Critical Update Patch, go to My Documents Folder, right-click on Install Patch, click Yes, Yes, No, Yes, Maybe, Yes, No, No, No, Definitely Not, then reboot, and twirl around three times while throwing salt behind your back and chanting "Alla-Malla-Kazoo." It's that simple.

1. To which of the following statements would the author most likely agree?
   (A) Microsoft is an eco-friendly company.
   (B) The next computer you purchase should be a Mac.
   (C) Bill Gates is sympathetic to the plight of hackers.
   (D) Throwing salt behind one's back will bring good luck.
   (E) Pornography is a necessary evil.

2. In this passage, which of the following statements does the author imply?
   I. The process of updating the Windows operating system is both unreliable and much too complicated.
   II. The Windows operating system is not secure.
   III. The Windows operating system is very "buggy," containing too many flaws.
   (A) I only
   (B) II only
   (C) I and III only
   (D) II and III only
   (E) I, II, and III

3. In line 2, "critical" most nearly means
   (A) nit-picking
   (B) life-threatening
   (C) disparaging
   (D) significant
   (E) analytical

4. According to experts, people who fail to update their Windows operating system with the latest software patch risk
   (A) having any personal information stored on their computer compromised
   (B) being blackmailed for looking at pornography
   (C) having their computer lock up
   (D) failing to follow Microsoft's warning
   (E) having their computer stolen

5. In this passage, one can infer that the most serious of the Windows operating system flaws is referred to as
   (A) critical
   (B) super-duper
   (C) quite serious
   (D) Orange
   (E) D'oh!

TYPES OF QUESTIONS

Questions on critical reading passages fall into one of three types:

1. Literal comprehension: These questions ask about specific information directly written in the passage.

2. Contextual meaning: These questions ask about the meaning of a specific word or phrase in the context of the passage.

3. True understanding: These questions test your true understanding of the passage and your ability to process what is written and interpret it.

Degree of Difficulty

Questions on passages, unlike questions for any other portion of the exam, do not progress from easy to medium to hard. It is quite possible for the first question on a particular passage to be the hardest and the last question to be the easiest.

HOW TO SOLVE CRITICAL READING PASSAGES

Some people read through the entire passage first before looking at the questions. Others look at the questions first and search through the passage to find the answer to each question. The first approach is more thorough, but it can take longer, and you may run out of time before you get to all the questions. The second approach gets to the questions much quicker, but if you don't read the passage first, you may not have a good enough overall understanding of the passage to answer all of the questions correctly.

A third approach is a combination of the first two approaches. Rather than read the entire passage first, maybe just read the first paragraph, the first sentence of each middle paragraph, and the final paragraph, to get a rough idea of the passage. Then go through the questions one by one and search through the passage to find the information you need to answer each question.

For short passages, it probably doesn't matter which way you go about it. For big-ass passages, knowing which strategy works best for you can save you a lot of time during the test. Your strategy may also depend on the type of passage and the types of questions about it. For example, if the passage is really tough and boring, and the questions mostly refer to specific line numbers, you probably want to get to the questions more quickly and hunt and peck for the answers in the passage. On the other hand, if the passage is relatively breezy or many questions ask you about the passage as a whole rather than specific line numbers, then you probably should read the passage in its entirety before you answer the questions.

Finally, keep in mind that questions on passages do not progress from easy to hard, so it may be advantageous to skip a question that looks difficult and come back to it later. DO NOT, however, skip back and forth between different passages, as you likely will forget one passage as soon as you read the next one. Answer all the questions you can on one passage and then move on to the next one. Come back to the questions you've skipped once you've answered all the other questions you can answer in the section.

Let's now take a closer look at the questions for our earlier passage and work through how to solve them.

---

1. To which of the following statements would the author most likely agree?
   (A) Microsoft is an eco-friendly company.
   (B) The next computer you purchase should be a Mac.
   (C) Bill Gates is sympathetic to the plight of hackers.
   (D) Throwing salt behind one's back will bring good luck.
   (E) Pornography is a necessary evil.

ANSWER: **B**

SOLUTION: This is a true understanding question. Based on what the author writes in the passage, you have to infer the author's opinion concerning the five statements listed in the answer choices.

Let's take a look at each one:

A. The passage doesn't say anything about the environment, one way or the other, so this cannot be the right answer.

B. The entire passage points out problems with Microsoft's operating system, and at the end of the first paragraph the author even uses the phrase "too stupid to buy a Mac." Based on the passage, it seems pretty clear that the author would agree that the next computer you purchase should be a Mac. This is very likely the correct answer, but just to be sure, we should quickly look at the other choices just in case.

C. The plight of hackers is not discussed in the passage.

D. Although the author mentions throwing salt behind one's back to bring good luck, such a mention is not made in a way to make us think the author actually believes in that superstition.

E. The passage seems to acknowledge that some people view pornography on their computer, but the author does not appear to pass any moral judgment on pornography.

THE CORRECT ANSWER IS (B).

2. In this passage, which of the following statements does the author imply?

    I. The process of updating the Windows operating system is both unreliable and much too complicated.

    II. The Windows operating system is not secure.

    III. The Windows operating system is very "buggy," containing too many flaws.

  (A) I only

  (B) II only

  (C) I and III only

  (D) II and III only

  (E) I, II, and III

ANSWER: **E**

SOLUTION: This is a true understanding question. Three statements are made, and you have to go through each statement and decide if it is implied by the author.

    I. The last paragraph implies that the Windows operating system is both unreliable and much too complicated.

    II. The first sentence in the second paragraph suggests that serious security flaws seem to occur all too often, thus implying that the Windows operating system is not secure.

    III. The first sentence in the second paragraph suggests that serious security flaws seem to occur all too often, thus implying that the Windows operating system is very "buggy."

THE CORRECT ANSWER IS (E).

---

3. In line 2, "critical" most nearly means

  (A) nit-picking

  (B) life-threatening

  (C) disparaging

  (D) significant

  (E) analytical

ANSWER: **D**

SOLUTION: This is a contextual meaning question. The word *critical* has several possible meanings and you need to figure out which one is being used within the passage. In this passage, the word *critical* is being used to mean *serious*. Microsoft has yet another serious flaw that needs fixing and in the meantime billions of us have to put up with their crappy software yet again. From the answer choices, the only one that means *serious* is *significant*.

THE CORRECT ANSWER IS (D).

4. According to experts, people who fail to update their Windows operating system with the latest software patch risk
   (A) having any personal information stored on their computer compromised
   (B) being blackmailed for looking at pornography
   (C) having their computer lock up
   (D) failing to follow Microsoft's warning
   (E) having their computer stolen

ANSWER: **A**

SOLUTION: This is a literal comprehension question. The information can be found directly in the passage, although the words might be paraphrased in the question or answer choices. To answer the question, first find where the information is located in the passage—the third paragraph of the passage in this case. Now which of the five answers is something that the experts say?

   A. The experts say that a hacker can "delete your data, eavesdrop on sensitive information, and even steal the porn straight off your hard drive." All of these are examples of having personal information stored on the computer compromised. This is most likely the correct answer, but let's quickly go through the other choices just in case.
   B. It is possible for a person to be blackmailed for looking at pornography, but the experts only mention the possibility of a person's pornography being *stolen*.
   C. It is possible for a person's computer to lock up, especially if they are using a Microsoft product, but this is not explicitly mentioned by the experts.
   D. It is true that people who don't install the patch are not following Microsoft's warning, but that doesn't have anything to do with the experts.
   E. No mention is made about the actual computer itself being stolen. Who would want to steal a PC when they can steal a Mac instead?

THE CORRECT ANSWER IS (A).

5. In this passage, one can infer that the most serious of the Windows operating system flaws is referred to as
   (A) critical
   (B) super-duper
   (C) quite serious
   (D) Orange
   (E) D'oh!

ANSWER: **E**

SOLUTION: This is a true understanding question. You have to infer from the passage which term refers to the most serious flaw. In the first sentence of the second paragraph, it seems that the author lists the flaws in increasing level of seriousness, so you can infer that the last one is the

most serious. The use of the phrase "of course" also suggests that "D'oh!" was a doozy of a flaw that people still remember from a year ago. The exclamation point is one further indication that "D'oh!" is the most serious of the flaws listed.
THE CORRECT ANSWER IS (E).

WAYS TO IMPROVE YOUR SCORE

1. Increase Your Vocabulary

Once again, if you increase your vocabulary, you will be able to understand any difficult words in both the passages and the questions and answer choices. You'll increase your chances of answering correctly and you'll also gain valuable exam time because you won't have to spend time trying to figure out what all the words mean.

Another great thing about knowing big, fancy words is that they're a great way to get someone to break up with you when you want to break up with them. Simply start using big words in every sentence around the person you want to dump and very quickly they'll find you so annoying they'll break up with you. No fuss, no muss.

2. Keep Track of Time

There are often many questions associated with a single passage. If you run out of time before making it to the last passage, you won't just miss one question, but ALL THE QUESTIONS ASSOCIATED WITH THAT PASSAGE. Be aware of the clock. Also, remember that questions on passages don't progress from easy to hard. DON'T WASTE ALL YOUR TIME ON ONE QUESTION! That statement is actually true for the entire test, but especially true for the critical reading passages.

3. Practice

Practice your strategy, especially with the big-ass passages. As you practice on more and more passages, you'll find the right strategy that works for you, and you'll also get a lot faster in the process. Many students run out of time in the Critical Reading sections of the test because they didn't practice their strategy on the big-ass passages.

Reality Check

Okay, so you probably won't ever see a Yo Momma joke on an official SAT* exam, and you probably won't read any passages with the word "D'oh!" in them either. However, everything you've just learned about the Critical Reading portion of the exam still applies to their lame-ass, boring sentences and their lame-ass, boring passages. If you master the approach to sentence completions, you will speed through them in no time at all. If you practice your technique for the critical reading passages, you'll ace those as well.

The Critical Reading practice sections will give you a chance to practice what you've learned and will more fully test your knowledge of the material you need to know for the Critical Reading portion of the exam. Feel free to jump to the Critical Reading practice sections at this point beginning on page 123, or save them until after you've gone through the Writing and Math reviews as well.

PART 3
WRITING

Writing Overview

The Writing portion of the SAT* exam consists of four types of questions:

- *Finding sentence errors*

- *Improving sentences*

- *Improving paragraphs*

- *The essay*

The exact breakdown looks like this:

WRITING: 3 SECTIONS	
TYPE OF QUESTIONS	**NO. OF QUESTIONS**
Finding sentence errors	18 questions
Improving sentences	25 questions
Improving paragraphs	6 questions
The essay	1 essay

TYPICAL SECTION BREAKDOWNS

25-MINUTE SECTION	1 ESSAY

25-MINUTE SECTION	35 QUESTIONS
11 improving sentences	11 questions
18 finding sentence errors	18 questions
1 improving paragraphs	6 questions

10-MINUTE SECTION	14 QUESTIONS
14 improving sentences	14 questions

Common Sentence Errors

The basic building block in writing is the sentence. A well-crafted sentence is clear, unambiguous, effective, and properly constructed, and it follows all the rules of standard written English. In the Writing portion of the exam, you will be asked to identify sentence errors, fix sentence errors, and write proper sentences of your own.

The best way to learn how to write a good sentence is to understand what makes a sentence bad. A thorough understanding of the following list of common sentence errors will greatly help you improve your test score. In the following chapters, we cover all the types of questions you will see in the Writing portion of the exam. The single best way to improve your score is to gain a thorough understanding of the common sentence errors described below.

SHIFTING VERB TENSES

BAD   After The Toddmeister polished off the keg, he passes out on the floor.

BETTER   After The Toddmeister polished off the keg, he <u>passed</u> out on the floor.

SHIFTING PRONOUNS

BAD   If you polish off a keg, one should try not to drunk dial your ex.

BETTER   If you polish off a keg, <u>you</u> should try not to drunk dial your ex.

LACK OF PARALLELISM

BAD   The Toddmeister polished off the keg, hit on Maria, vomited on her shoes, and passing out on the floor was something he also did.

BETTER   The Toddmeister polished off the keg, hit on Maria, vomited on her shoes, and <u>passed out on the floor</u>.

MIXING UP SINGULAR AND PLURAL—NOUNS

BAD   The Toddmeister and The Brettmeister wish to become a fraternity brother.

BETTER   The Toddmeister and The Brettmeister wish to become <u>fraternity brothers</u>.

MIXING UP SINGULAR AND PLURAL—VERBS

BAD   The Toddmeister and The Brettmeister thinks joining a fraternity will help them score with the ladies.

BETTER   The Toddmeister and The Brettmeister <u>think</u> joining a fraternity will help them score with the ladies.

MIXING UP ADJECTIVES AND ADVERBS

BAD   The Toddmeister was obviously wasted, so Maria acted cautious when he approached her.

BETTER   The Toddmeister was obviously wasted, so Maria acted <u>cautiously</u> when he approached her.

MIXING UP WORDS—DICTION ERRORS[1]

BAD   The Toddmeister suggested that he and Maria should hook up all ready because he was now single and she was so fine.

BETTER   The Toddmeister suggested that he and Maria should hook up <u>already</u> because he was now single and she was so fine.

[1.] See Appendix for a list of common diction errors.

IMPROPER PRONOUN CASE

BAD   The Toddmeister said that him and Maria might as well hook up because he would tell everyone they did anyway.

BETTER   The Toddmeister said that <u>he</u> and Maria might as well hook up because he would tell everyone they did anyway.

IDIOM ERRORS[2]

BAD   The Toddmeister tried to apologize to Maria by comparing her breasts with those of a Playboy model, and then he yakked on her shoes.

BETTER   The Toddmeister tried to apologize to Maria by <u>comparing</u> her breasts <u>to</u> those of a Playboy model, and then he yakked on her shoes.

COMMA SPLICE—SUBORDINATE CLAUSES

BAD   Maria had barf all over her Jimmy Choos, her shoes were ruined.

STILL NOT GOOD   Maria had barf all over her Jimmy Choos, and her shoes were ruined.

BETTER   Maria had barf all over her Jimmy Choos<u>;</u> her shoes were ruined.

COMMA SPLICE—COORDINATING CONJUNCTION

BAD   Maria had barf all over her Jimmy Choos, she left the party in a huff.

BETTER   Maria had barf all over her Jimmy Choos, <u>so</u> she left the party in a huff.

---

[2] See Appendix for a list of common idioms.

MISPLACED MODIFIERS

BAD   Maria decided she'd rather be a lesbian on her way out the door.

BETTER On her way out the door, Maria decided she'd rather be a lesbian.

DANGLING PARTICIPLES

BAD   Waving wildly, the cab stopped to pick up Maria and her new friend Daphne.

BETTER Waving wildly, Maria and her new friend Daphne were able to get the cab to stop and pick them up.

AMBIGUITY

BAD   The Brettmeister told The Toddmeister to keep chugging because for the fraternity they only admit a few new pledges each year.

BETTER The Brettmeister told The Toddmeister to keep chugging because the fraternity only admits a few new pledges each year.

TOO WORDY

BAD   It took ten rounds in order to find the person who won in the drinking challenge that was the final one.

BETTER It took ten rounds to find a winner in the final drinking challenge.

PASSIVE VERBS

BAD   When you throw up and pass out, your drinking probably should be stopped.

BETTER When you throw up and pass out, you should probably stop drinking.

MISSING SUBJECTS

BAD   If your keg is empty while seeing someone passed out on the floor, it should not be refilled until after checking to see if that person is okay.

BETTER   If your keg is empty <u>and you see</u> someone passed out on the floor, <u>your keg</u> should not be refilled until after <u>you</u> check to see if that person is okay.

SENTENCE FRAGMENTS

BAD   When The Toddmeister looked as though he wasn't breathing.

BETTER   The Toddmeister looked as though he wasn't breathing.

MODIFIER COMPARISON ERRORS

BAD   Of all the fraternity pledges, The Toddmeister suffered the greater degree of alcohol poisoning.

BETTER   Of all the fraternity pledges, The Toddmeister suffered the <u>greatest</u> degree of alcohol poisoning.

LOGICAL COMPARISON ERRORS

BAD   The Toddmeister required more urgent medical attention than The Brettmeister's sickness.

BETTER   The Toddmeister required more urgent medical attention than The Brettmeister.

Finding Sentence Errors

In these questions, you're given sentences that may contain an error and you have to find the error (if there is one).

For example:

1. <u>Seconds after</u> receiving the 911 call, the operator
      A
    <u>dispatched</u> two <u>emergency medical technician</u> to the
      B   C
    Kappa Omega Kappa <u>fraternity</u>. <u>No error</u>
                        D   E

Specific words or parts of each sentence are underlined, and if there's an error in the sentence, it comes from one of the underlined parts. You have to find which underlined part of the sentence contains an error, or determine that there is no error and the sentence is correct. Each underlined portion of the sentence is assigned a letter, from A to D, and every sentence is followed by the words "No error," which is assigned the letter E. So if the sentence is correct, choose E.

HOW TO SOLVE FINDING SENTENCE ERRORS

Keep in mind the common sentence errors covered in the previous chapter, and try to determine if any of those errors occur in the sentence.

Let's take a look at our sample question:

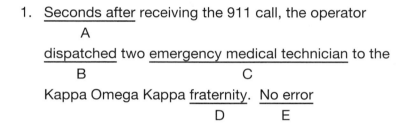

1. <u>Seconds after</u> receiving the 911 call, the operator
      A
    <u>dispatched</u> two <u>emergency medical technician</u> to the
      B   C
    Kappa Omega Kappa <u>fraternity</u>. <u>No error</u>
                        D   E

ANSWER: **C**

SOLUTION: The sentence error is one of mixing up singular and plural. The operator dispatched two emergency medical *technicians*—plural, not two emergency medical *technician*—singular. THE CORRECT ANSWER IS (C).

When you examine the sentence for errors, be especially careful if the sentence has a long separation caused by modifiers. For example:

2. <u>Loading</u> The Toddmeister onto a gurney, the emergency
        A

    medical technicians, <u>who happened</u> to be Kappa Omega
                      B

    Kappa brothers <u>themselves</u> and the winning team of the
                 C

    2000 Chug-a-thon, <u>was relieved</u> to see that the
                  D

    championship drinking trophy was still out on display.

    <u>No error</u>
      E

ANSWER: **D**

SOLUTION: It may look like "was relieved" (singular) fits together with "winning team" (singular) but that's the wrong pairing. The words "was relieved" are supposed to match up with "emergency medical technicians," which is plural. So it should actually be "were relieved" instead. In other words, it should read "the emergency medical technicians . . . were relieved to see that the championship drinking trophy was still out on display." The difficulty in this question comes from the fact that "emergency medical technicians" and "was relieved" are separated really far by a lengthy modifier. Be very careful around such sentences.
THE CORRECT ANSWER IS (D).

Here's another tricky sentence:

3. After The Toddmeister was taken away, the fraternity

    president, <u>as well as</u> the remaining pledges, <u>were</u>
             A   B

    <u>insistent</u> that the party <u>should</u> continue. <u>No error</u>
       C   D   E

ANSWER: **B**

SOLUTION: It may look like "remaining pledges" (plural) fits together with "were insistent" (plural), but that's the wrong pairing. The subject is "the fraternity president," which is singular. So it should actually be "was insistent" instead. In other words, it should read "the fraternity president . . . was insistent that the party should continue." "As well as the remaining pledges" is separate from "the fraternity president" and is not part of the subject.
THE CORRECT ANSWER IS (B).

A FEW THINGS TO REMEMBER

- The non-underlined portions of the sentence are correct, so use them to guide you to the right answer. In our first sample question, the word "two" was not underlined, so that told us we needed two technicians, not two technician.

- Read the sentences slowly, because your brain can automatically correct errors in your head. Again, in our first sample question, if you read the sentence too quickly, your brain may automatically read the word "technicians" instead of "technician," so you may think there's no error when there is one.

- There is at most one error in the sentence. There are never two or more errors in the same sentence.

- If you have a gut feeling for which underlined part is incorrect, but you don't remember what specific type of sentence error it is, go with your gut. For these questions you only need to locate the error—you don't need to know exactly what type of error it is.

Improving Sentences

In these questions, a portion of each sentence (or even the entire sentence) is underlined and you have to choose the best way to improve the sentence.

For example:

1. In the ambulance, the emergency medical technicians yelled at The Toddmeister to not give up on them, <u>administering CPR, and applying a defibrillator</u>.
   (A) administering CPR, and applying a defibrillator
   (B) administered CPR, and applying a defibrillator
   (C) administering CPR, and a defibrillator they applied
   (D) administered CPR, and applied a defibrillator
   (E) CPR they administered, and a defibrillator they applied

Choice (A) is always an exact repeat of the underlined part of the sentence, so if you think the sentence was fine exactly the way it was, you should choose (A) as your answer.

HOW TO SOLVE IMPROVING SENTENCES

Again, it is important to keep in mind the common sentence errors covered in the previous chapters, and to determine if any of those errors occur in the sentence.

Let's take a look at our sample question:

---

1. In the ambulance, the emergency medical technicians yelled at The Toddmeister to not give up on them, <u>administering CPR, and applying a defibrillator</u>.
   (A) administering CPR, and applying a defibrillator
   (B) administered CPR, and applying a defibrillator
   (C) administering CPR, and a defibrillator they applied
   (D) administered CPR, and applied a defibrillator
   (E) CPR they administered, and a defibrillator they applied

ANSWER: **D**

SOLUTION: The sentence is lacking a parallel structure. "Yelled" is past tense, so the underlined portion of the sentence should follow the same pattern. It should be "administered CPR" and "applied a defibrillator."
THE CORRECT ANSWER IS (D).

A FEW THINGS TO REMEMBER

- The non-underlined portion of the sentence is correct, so use it to guide you to the right answer. In our previous example, the word "yelled" was not underlined, so it was a key word telling us that the other verbs should be in the past tense as well.

- Read each choice as part of the entire sentence. Don't just read the answer choice by itself—the answer choice might sound right on its own, but not be right in the context of the rest of the sentence that wasn't underlined.

Improving Paragraphs

For these questions, you're given a rough draft of a passage and you have to answer questions on how to improve the passage. The questions on the passage are all about ways to improve specific sentences in the passage or how to improve the passage as a whole.

For example:

Questions 1–6 are based on the following passage, the first draft of a eulogy.

(1) Ladies and Gentlemen, today we have lost a most righteous and gnarly dude, taken from us way too soon. (2) The Toddmeister is, simply put, the most heinous, sick-ass, wicked-cool person on the face of the planet. (3) He was also my best friend.

(4) Man, who can forget the time when, on a dare, you nude-boarded down Darcy Street, rode the handrail, and attempted a hang eleven. (5) You fell right on your gnards; I couldn't stop laughing for a week. (6) Dude, remember Spring Break in Aruba when that weird bearded dude slipped you some ridiculous acid and you tripped so hard you thought you could fly? (7) You busted two ribs and punctured a lung. (8) Did that stop you? (9) No, you were right back there partying the very next night, pounding them down with the rest of us. (10) I'll bet you're chugging with the Big Man himself, and teaching him a thing or two while you're at it. (11) You friggin' rock, dude! (12) Ladies and Gentlemen, The Toddmeister may no longer be with us in flesh, but he most excellently lives on in spirit. (13) Wherever there's a bitchin' rad party, The Toddmeister will be there. (14) Wherever there's a smooth keg that needs tapping, The Toddmeister will be there. (15) Let us lift our voices as we lift our steins at this time.

1. In context, which is the best way to deal with sentence 2 (reproduced as follows)?

    The Toddmeister is, simply put, the most heinous, sick-ass, wicked-cool person on the face of the planet.

    (A) Leave it as is.
    (B) Insert "who has ever lived" before "on the face of the planet".
    (C) Delete "the face of".
    (D) Delete "simply put".
    (E) Change "is" to "was".

2. Which of the following would be the best sentence to insert at the beginning of the second paragraph?
    (A) Let me tell you a little story about The Toddmeister.
    (B) The Toddmeister was always a jokester.
    (C) When I remember The Toddmeister, I remember good times.
    (D) I would like to tell you all why we should honor The Toddmeister.
    (E) The Toddmeister was an incredible athlete.

3. In context, which is the best way to revise and combine sentences 7 and 8 (reproduced as follows)?

    You busted two ribs and punctured a lung. Did that stop you?

    (A) You busted two ribs and punctured a lung, but did that stop you?
    (B) You busted two ribs and punctured a lung, did that stop you?
    (C) You busted two ribs and punctured a lung; but did that stop you?
    (D) You busted two ribs, punctured a lung, and did that stop you?
    (E) Did it stop you while you busted two ribs and punctured a lung?

4. What should be done with sentence 10 (reproduced as follows)?

    I'll bet you're chugging with the Big Man himself, and teaching him a thing or two while you're at it.

    (A) Leave it as is.
    (B) Insert "Right now," at the beginning.
    (C) Add ", you dog" at the end.
    (D) Move it before sentence 9.
    (E) Delete it.

5. Which of the following is best to add after sentence 15?
   (A) Amen.
   (B) My name is Ryan, and I'm an alcoholic.
   (C) To The Toddmeister, a scholarship will be named in your honor.
   (D) Dude, this keg's for you.
   (E) Let's go bury someone.

6. At what point in the passage is it most logical to begin a new, third paragraph?
   (A) After sentence 5
   (B) After sentence 8
   (C) After sentence 9
   (D) After sentence 10
   (E) After sentence 11

HOW TO SOLVE IMPROVING PARAGRAPHS

The passages in this section are usually short and you shouldn't worry about the time it takes to read the passage. Read the passage first so that you have a good overall grasp of what the author is trying to say.

Once again, it is important to keep in mind the common sentence errors covered in the previous chapters, but this time you also need to keep in mind paragraph structure and how the sentences should logically fit together.

Let's take a closer look at the questions for our sample passage and work through how to solve them.

---

1. In context, which is the best way to deal with sentence 2 (reproduced as follows)?

The Toddmeister is, simply put, the most heinous, sick-ass, wicked-cool person on the face of the planet.

   (A) Leave it as is.
   (B) Insert "who has ever lived" before "on the face of the planet".
   (C) Delete "the face of".
   (D) Delete "simply put".
   (E) Change "is" to "was".

ANSWER: **E**
SOLUTION: The sentence may be structurally correct on its own, but we should remember that it's part of a paragraph. The Toddmeister (being deceased) is referred to in the past

tense in both sentence 1 and sentence 3. He should also be referred to in the past tense in sentence 2.
THE CORRECT ANSWER IS (E).

---

2. Which of the following would be the best sentence to insert at the beginning of the second paragraph?
    (A) Let me tell you a little story about The Toddmeister.
    (B) The Toddmeister was always a jokester.
    (C) When I remember The Toddmeister, I remember good times.
    (D) I would like to tell you all why we should honor The Toddmeister.
    (E) The Toddmeister was an incredible athlete.

ANSWER: **C**
SOLUTION: The second paragraph describes some fond memories the author had concerning The Toddmeister. The point is not that he was a jokester or an athlete, so we can eliminate (B) and (E). The point of the paragraph is not to convince people to honor The Toddmeister either, so (D) can be eliminated. Both (A) and (C) fit, but (A) does not flow well into sentence 4, and in fact the author tells more than one story about The Toddmeister, so (A) can be eliminated as well. On the other hand, (C) flows well into sentence 4 and serves to introduce the author's fond recollections.
THE CORRECT ANSWER IS (C).

---

3. In context, which is the best way to revise and combine sentences 7 and 8 (reproduced as follows)?

    You busted two ribs and punctured a lung. Did that stop you?

    (A) You busted two ribs and punctured a lung, but did that stop you?
    (B) You busted two ribs and punctured a lung, did that stop you?
    (C) You busted two ribs and punctured a lung; but did that stop you?
    (D) You busted two ribs, punctured a lung, and did that stop you?
    (E) Did it stop you while you busted two ribs and punctured a lung?

ANSWER: **A**
SOLUTION: Think about what the author is trying to say. Here, the author's point is that even though The Toddmeister got hurt, he didn't let it stop him from partying hard the next day. The only answer choice that is properly written and conveys this idea is (A).

Knowing the common sentence errors can come in handy to eliminate some of the answer choices. For example, (B) is a comma splice and (C) incorrectly uses a semicolon followed by a conjunction.
THE CORRECT ANSWER IS (A).

4. What should be done with sentence 10 (reproduced as follows)?

I'll bet you're chugging with the Big Man himself, and teaching him a thing or two while you're at it.

(A) Leave it as is.
(B) Insert "Right now," at the beginning.
(C) Add ", you dog" at the end.
(D) Move it before sentence 9.
(E) Delete it.

ANSWER: **B**

SOLUTION: The sentence on its own may look correct, but remember that it's part of a paragraph. The sentence needs to flow smoothly from the preceding sentence and it also needs to flow smoothly into the subsequent one. Currently, there is a slight disconnection from the previous sentence. The verb tense in sentence 9 is different from the verb tense in sentence 10, so a modifier as in (B) would help to make the two sentences flow together.

Choice (C) makes no real meaningful change and (D) is clearly incorrect because sentence 10 does not answer the question posed in sentence 8. Choice (E) would also fix the tenses problem, but at the cost of losing sentence 10 in its entirety. It would be better to fix sentence 10 than delete it entirely.

THE CORRECT ANSWER IS (B).

---

5. Which of the following is best to add after sentence 15?
(A) Amen.
(B) My name is Ryan, and I'm an alcoholic.
(C) To The Toddmeister, a scholarship will be named in your honor.
(D) Dude, this keg's for you.
(E) Let's go bury someone.

ANSWER: **D**

SOLUTION: Consider the passage as a whole, the sentences leading up to sentence 15, and sentence 15 in particular. The author is asking people to lift up their voices as they lift up their steins—in other words, he is about to lead them in a toast. Choice (D) is the most appropriate toast that fits into the passage as a whole.

THE CORRECT ANSWER IS (D).

6. At what point in the passage is it most logical to begin a new, third paragraph?

    (A) After sentence 5
    (B) After sentence 8
    (C) After sentence 9
    (D) After sentence 10
    (E) After sentence 11

ANSWER: **E**

SOLUTION: A good place to start a new paragraph is at a point where a change in direction takes place or a new topic is started. Choices (A), (B), (C), and (D) would all disrupt the flow of the passage by starting a new paragraph while still in the middle of the same topic. Choice (E), on the other hand, provides a change in direction, and is a good place to begin a new paragraph to conclude the eulogy.

THE CORRECT ANSWER IS (E).

The Essay

The essay is always the first section on the SAT* exam. You will be asked to write an essay in response to a question. This question will not be on any specific topic you're expected to study, and there won't be a specific right or wrong answer.

For example:

"The Partridge Family were neither partridges nor a family."
—Mike Myers as Linda Richman, "Coffee Talk"

ASSIGNMENT: Is pretending to be something you're not always wrong? Write an essay to describe your point of view on this subject. Use examples and logical reasoning to support your position.

The essay is graded using what they call "holistic scoring," which means they give you a score based on the overall impression of the essay, not based on any specific point-by-point breakdown. Two independent readers score the essay from 1 to 6 and the two scores are added together. (If the scores from the two readers differ by more than one point, then a supervisor scores the essay, and the score from the supervisor is doubled.)

HOW TO APPROACH THE ESSAY

In your test booklet quickly create a short outline for your essay. Use point form to list your viewpoint, the main idea for each paragraph, and the conclusion. You only have 25 minutes to write the entire essay, so don't waste too much time on a detailed outline. Only spend enough time to get you started on what you want to say and to give you a basic direction to follow. Even though this outline won't be graded, it will be worth creating because it will help you write a better and more focused essay.

When you have a broad outline, just dive in. Don't worry so much about making things look perfect and don't worry about your handwriting. As far as handwriting size goes, avoid writing so small that it looks as if you've written a lot less than you actually have, but otherwise don't worry about it. In terms of legibility, make it legible, but don't worry if it doesn't look perfect. You can even cross out words and make corrections as you go along. It's much more important that the essay is well written than written well.

Present your viewpoint logically. Don't write just to fill up space, and don't meander all over the place. Shoot for a minimum of three paragraphs. Four or five substantial and well-written paragraphs should give you a pretty high score. Have a beginning, a middle, and a conclusion.

Examples taken from your real life can be used to support your position, but if you really can't think of examples from your real life, *just make stuff up*. Again, they are testing your ability to write a logical essay—they could care less about you and your actual real-life problems. There are also no right or wrong viewpoints, only well-written or poorly-written essays. Having said that, it may not be a great idea to argue that "they should bring back slavery" or "Hitler was a great guy," and you should probably also leave out that story about "the hobo you killed just for fun."

Finally, if time permits, try to give yourself a few minutes at the end to review your essay and catch mistakes or make improvements.

A FEW THINGS TO REMEMBER

- Make sure to include some complex sentences, not just short and simple ones having one subject and one verb.

- Be specific. Don't write in vague generalities—give examples from your real life or things you've read or seen or otherwise experienced.

- Avoid common sentence errors. Use everything you've learned in the previous chapters about sentences and paragraphs.

- You can make a reference back to any specific quote given in the question if it helps your essay, but don't feel like you have to.

- Make sure your essay is about the topic given in the question. If you write an off-topic essay, you get a score of zero.

- Remember to use a pencil and not a pen, and remember to write on your answer sheet and not your test booklet.

- If you aren't used to writing essays, you'll need to practice beforehand. DO NOT make the first essay you write be the one you write during the exam. Now, some people actually prepare and memorize an essay in advance, hoping they'll be able to use it during the test. It might work if you're lucky, but it might also backfire if the question you are asked has nothing to do with your prepackaged essay and you get flustered trying to make it fit. It's better to practice writing a few essays, so you'll be prepared for whatever is thrown at you. Why don't you try writing one right now—say, the question we gave you at the beginning of the chapter?

Reality Check

What are the chances you'll see a sentence about The Toddmeister on the real SAT* exam? Pretty much zero. It's too late, though, because you've already just learned a whole ton about the Writing portion of the exam.

Yes, they'll give you retardedly boring sentences and paragraphs because they have no sense of humor and they're dead inside, but you'll know how to approach these boring sentences and paragraphs because you now know the common sentence errors and how to fix them and you also know how to improve the structure of a paragraph. Finally, you've also learned a bunch of great tips to help you write a killer essay.

The Writing practice sections will give you a chance to practice what you've learned and will more fully test your knowledge of the material you need to know for the Writing portion of the exam. Feel free to jump to the Writing practice sections beginning on page 145 at this point, or save them until after you've gone through the Critical Reading and Math reviews as well.

PART 4
MATH

Math Overview

Yeah, yeah, math is hard. We know. We know. Would you rather learn it with boring questions about bakers and builders, or with questions about Lindsay Lohan and Angelina Jolie? Thought so.

The areas of math that you need to know for the SAT* exam are:

- *Numbers and operations*

- *Algebra*

- *Functions*

- *Geometry*

- *Elementary statistics and probability*

The exact breakdown of the Math portion looks like this:

MATH: 3 SECTIONS	
TYPE OF QUESTIONS	**NO. OF QUESTIONS**
Multiple choice	44 questions
Grid-ins	10 questions

TYPICAL SECTION BREAKDOWNS

25-MINUTE SECTION	20 QUESTIONS
20 multiple choice	20 questions

25-MINUTE SECTION	18 QUESTIONS
8 multiple choice	8 questions
10 grid-ins	10 questions

20-MINUTE SECTION	16 QUESTIONS
16 multiple choice	16 questions

GRID-INS

Grid-in questions have no answers to choose from—you have to solve for the answer directly and fill in the corresponding circles of the answer box, also known as a "grid."

Here are two examples of grids:

GRIDS (magnified)

- Answers can be filled in as whole numbers, fractions, or decimals. For example, if the answer you want to fill in is $\frac{3}{2}$, you can fill it in as either 3/2 or 1.5. Don't use mixed fractions (for example, $1\frac{1}{2}$ would be read as $\frac{11}{2}$).

- You can start at either the left-most column or right-most column. Leave any unused columns blank.

- If decimal answers go beyond the grid, you can round the number or truncate, but you have to use the entire grid. For example, $\frac{2}{3}$ can be filled in as either 2/3, .667, or .666, but not as .67.

- The top handwritten portion of the grid is not actually scored. You HAVE TO fill in the circles.

- Notice how there is no way to fill in a negative number. In fact, all answers to grid-in questions will be between 0 and 9999. If you get a different answer to one of these questions, you know you did it wrong.

- Some grid-in questions can have multiple correct answers, in which case you can just pick any of the correct ones and fill that answer into the grid. We'll see an example of this in one of the sample questions later in the chapter.

DIFFICULTY LEVEL

In each section, questions generally start easy and get progressively harder. This is true unless a section contains both multiple-choice and grid-in questions, in which case the questions go from easy to hard within the multiple-choice portion and then start again from easy to hard within the grid-in portion.

How to Get the Right Answer When You Don't Even Understand the Question

The SAT* exam tests not only your knowledge of basic math concepts, but also your general reasoning skills. Reasoning skills can actually come in very handy because there are two general methods that you can use to find the right answer to a question even if you don't fully understand the question.

In fact, these two methods can be so useful that they are often treated as "secret insider tricks" by unscrupulous tutoring companies so they can charge you outrageous fees. They'll try to scare you by telling you that only *they* know these secrets to the exam and, if you give them thousands and thousands of dollars, they'll teach you how to "outsmart" the exam. Hey, if you're super rich and money doesn't mean anything to you, go for it. For the rest of us, buy this book and tell those tutoring companies where they can shove it.

Should you try to learn the basic math inside and out, and not just rely on these tricks? Absolutely. Anyone telling you that all you need to know are these "tricks" is doing you a great disservice. However, knowing when and how to use these two reasoning methods, together with knowing the basic math concepts, will go a very long way to increasing your math score.

METHOD 1—PLUGGING IN ANSWERS

This method is useless for the grid-in questions, but can be extremely useful for the multiple-choice questions. For multiple-choice questions, there's one thing you know with absolute certainty before even reading the question, and that is that *one of the five answers is the correct one*. Therefore, you can often work backwards from the answers, plugging them in to see which one is correct. For example:

1. Let m be the number of times Norbert gets pantsed during gym class and let n be the number of times Eugene gets pantsed during gym class. If m and n are positive integers and $m^2 - n^2 = 5$, what is the value of n?

   (A) 6
   (B) 5
   (C) 4
   (D) 3
   (E) 2

SOLUTION: This might look really hard on first glance. Suppose you're stuck. What can you do? Rather than throwing in the towel, or blind guessing, let's reason it out by plugging in the answers and working backward.

The Plugging In Answers Method:

Let's take each answer one by one, let n equal that answer, plug n into the equation $m^2 - n^2 = 5$, and solve for m. Because the question says m is a positive integer, our solution for m had better come out to be a positive integer or else we know that's the wrong answer.

   (A) If $n = 6$, then $m^2 - 36 = 5$, so the positive solution is $m = \sqrt{41}$, which is not an integer. Therefore, (A) is incorrect.

   (B) If $n = 5$, then $m^2 - 25 = 5$, so the positive solution is $m = \sqrt{30}$, which is not an integer. Therefore, (B) is incorrect.

   (C) If $n = 4$, then $m^2 - 16 = 5$, so the positive solution is $m = \sqrt{21}$, which is not an integer. Therefore, (C) is incorrect.

   (D) If $n = 3$, then $m^2 - 9 = 5$, so the positive solution is $m = \sqrt{14}$, which is not an integer. Therefore, (D) is incorrect.

   (E) If $n = 2$, then $m^2 - 4 = 5$, so the positive solution is $m = \sqrt{9} = 3$, which is a positive integer. (E) is correct!

By the way, here's the direct math solution:

$m^2 - n^2$ can be factored as $(m + n)(m - n)$, so

$$(m + n)(m - n) = 5$$

Because *m* and *n* are both positive integers, this means that

$$m + n = 5 \text{ and } m - n = 1$$

which are two equations with two unknowns that can be solved to obtain *m* = 3 and *n* = 2.

THE CORRECT ANSWER IS (E).

The answers are often listed in order from lowest to highest, or highest to lowest, so it can sometimes save you a bit of time if you start from answer choice (C). Sometimes you can work out if you need to go higher or lower, in which case you can save a little time by starting with (C). That wasn't the case in our sample question above, but it is true for some questions.

METHOD 2—PLUGGING IN NUMBERS

Some questions can have a number of different variables in them, all with different letters, which can make the questions look very confusing. In cases like these it may be easier to plug in specific numbers for the variables and work it through with those specific numbers. For example:

---

2. The price of steroids is *d* dollars for *f* fluid ounces of Winstrol and each fluid ounce of Winstrol can be used to make *s* syringes. In terms of *d*, *f*, and *s*, what is the dollar cost of steroids required to make one syringe?

   (A) $\frac{d}{fs}$

   (B) $\frac{ds}{f}$

   (C) $\frac{fs}{d}$

   (D) $\frac{df}{s}$

   (E) fds

SOLUTION: Suppose you see all these letters, *d*, *f*, and *s*, and just get confused and flustered. You ask yourself, "Why can't they give me numbers instead of all these stupid letters?" Well, guess what? You can use numbers if you want to. If the answer is true for any *d*, *f*, and *s*, then it is true for any specific numbers that you assign to *d*, *f*, and *s*. So it is true for *d* = 1, *f* = 2, and *s* = 3 for example, or $d = 5, f = 1$, and $s = 10$, or any other numbers that you want to assign them. So if it's difficult for you to work with letters, use numbers instead.

The Plugging In Numbers Method:

Let's let $d = 1, f = 2$, and $s = 3$. Then it costs 1 dollar to make 2 fluid ounces of Winstrol, and each fluid ounce makes 3 syringes. That means it costs 1 dollar to make $(2)(3) = 6$ syringes. So the cost of each syringe is $\frac{1}{6}$th of a dollar. Now let's plug our numbers into each answer choice to see which answer choice gives us $\frac{1}{6}$.

(A) $\frac{d}{fs} = \frac{1}{6}$

(B) $\frac{ds}{f} = \frac{3}{2}$

(C) $\frac{fs}{d} = 6$

(D) $\frac{df}{s} = \frac{2}{3}$

(E) $fds = 6$

THE CORRECT ANSWER IS (A)!

Were $d = 1, f = 2$, and $s = 3$ magic numbers? No—we could have used any set of numbers. We just picked low numbers to make it easy for us to do the math. We also made each number different from each other, to help us distinguish between the five answer choices. For example, if we let $d, f,$ and s all equal 1, all of the answer choices would have equaled 1 as well, so we still wouldn't know which answer was right. If it ever happens that two answer choices work out to be the same, just assign different numbers to the variables and do it all over again.

By the way, here's the direct math solution:

Using a sort of shorthand, we can write

$$d \text{ dollars} = f \text{ fluid ounces}$$

and

$$1 \text{ fluid ounce} = s \text{ syringes}$$

Therefore

$$d \text{ dollars} = f \text{ fluid ounces}$$
$$= f(s \text{ syringes})$$
$$= fs \text{ syringes}$$

which means that

$$1 \text{ syringe} = \frac{d}{fs} \text{ dollars}$$

In our shorthand, the equal signs denote an equivalency between the different objects. For example, f fluid ounces "costs" d dollars, or one fluid ounce "makes" s syringes. Keep track of the object types (dollars, ounces, syringes) to avoid confusion.

Common Types of Math Questions

Let's now go through, using examples, a bunch of the common types of math questions on the exam. This section, together with the practice sections found later in the book, provide an excellent review of most of the major math concepts and particularly how they tend to be tested on the SAT* exam. However, this section is not meant to be a 100 percent complete in-depth review of every math concept and every math question they can test you on (which would actually be impossible to do). If you find that you don't understand a particular concept listed in this section and need to learn more about it, you should consult your favorite math textbook, your teacher, or the math review section in *The Official SAT Study Guide*.

ALGEBRAIC EQUATIONS—SOLVE FOR *x*

Many problems fall under this category. You're given an algebraic equation and you simply have to solve for *x* (or *y* or *z* or whatever other letter they use). For example:

---

1. Let *x* equal the number of America's Next Top Models it takes to change a lightbulb. If $2(x - 3) = 16$, what is the value of *x*?

    (A) $\dfrac{13}{2}$

    (B) $\dfrac{19}{2}$

    (C) 8

    (D) 11

    (E) 19

SOLUTION:

$$2(x - 3) = 16$$

Divide both sides by 2 to get

$$x - 3 = 8$$

and then add 3 to both sides to get

$$x = 11$$

It takes 11 America's Next Top Models to change a lightbulb—1 to bitch to the cameras about a broken light, and 10 to look really fierce.

THE CORRECT ANSWER IS (D).

ANOTHER APPROACH

You can use the Plugging In Answers approach for this question as well. Plugging in (D), we get $2(11 - 3)$, which does equal 16, so we know the answer is (D).

ALGEBRAIC EQUATIONS—SOLVE FOR *x* IN TERMS OF OTHER SYMBOLS

You're given an algebraic equation and you have to again solve for *x*, but this time there are other letters in the equation. These questions may look difficult, but really they're the same as the regular solving for *x* questions, only with letters instead of numbers. For example:

---

2. Let *x* equal the number of dudes it takes to change a lightbulb.
   If $2(x - s) = t$, what is the value of *x* in terms of *s* and *t*?

   (A) $\dfrac{t - s}{2}$

   (B) $\dfrac{t + s}{2}$

   (C) $\dfrac{t - 2s}{2}$

   (D) $\dfrac{t + 2s}{2}$

   (E) $t + s$

SOLUTION: Notice how we'll manipulate the equation exactly as if *s* and *t* are numbers, so never let the letters confuse you.

$$2(x - s) = t$$

Expand to get

$$2x - 2s = t$$

Now move the $2s$ over to the other side to get

$$2x = t + 2s$$

And finally divide both sides by 2 to get

$$x = \frac{t + 2s}{2}$$

It takes $\frac{t + 2s}{2}$ dudes to change a lightbulb—one to change the bulb and the rest to point and say "Dude!"

THE CORRECT ANSWER IS (D).

ANOTHER APPROACH

You can use the Plugging In Numbers approach for this question if you get confused with all the letters. Pick numbers for s and t—let's say $s = 1$ and $t = 2$. Then $2(x - 1) = 2$ can be solved to get $x = 2$. If we plug our values for s and t into the answer choices, we find that only (D) gives us an answer of 2.

ALGEBRAIC EQUATIONS—DON'T SOLVE FOR x

Sometimes they'll give you a question where it looks like they haven't given you enough information to solve for x, and so it looks impossible. However, usually the trick is that the question doesn't ask you to solve for x, but to solve for something else that they *did* give you enough information to solve. You can't solve for x, but you can still answer the question. For example:

---

3. Let x equal the number of bipolars it takes to change a lightbulb.
   Let y equal the number of narcissists it takes to change a lightbulb.
   Let z equal the number of psychiatrists it takes to change a lightbulb.
   If $2x + y + z = 11$, what is the value of $4x + 2y + 2z - 3$?
   (A) 19
   (B) 22
   (C) 25
   (D) 33
   (E) 41

SOLUTION: Don't get confused even though the question doesn't give you enough information to solve individually for x or y or z. Although you don't know what x or y or z are individually, you do know that $2x + y + z = 11$ and this is enough to solve the question in this case. For a question like this, always look for how the information they give you relates to the thing they ask you to solve.

In this case:

$$4x + 2y + 2z - 3 = 2(2x + y + z) - 3$$
$$= 2(11) - 3$$
$$= 19$$

THE CORRECT ANSWER IS (A).

As far as the number of bipolars or narcissists or psychiatrists it takes to change a lightbulb, we can't say for sure, but we imagine the process involves the psychiatrists holding the bipolars back from sticking their fingers in the light socket and the narcissists being too preoccupied looking at themselves in the mirror to notice.

WORD PROBLEMS

Many questions are written in word form instead of mathematical symbols. For these questions, your first step is to translate the question into a mathematical equation. For example:

---

4. If 3 less than 4 times the number of calories in Nicole Richie's dinner is equal to 30 more than the same number, what is the number?

SOLUTION: Let x equal the number of calories in Nicole Richie's dinner. Then:

$$4x - 3 = x + 30$$
$$3x = 33$$
$$x = 11$$

THE CORRECT ANSWER IS 11.

   Nicole must have decided to binge tonight.

---

5. Charles had 505 minutes before the start of his history final. The amount of time he spent studying for the final was one-hundredth the time he spent playing *World of Warcraft*. How many minutes did he spend studying for the history final?

SOLUTION: Let x equal the number of minutes Charles spent studying for the history final. Then the number of minutes he spent playing *World of Warcraft* is 100x. The total time given was 505 minutes. Therefore,

$$x + 100x = 505$$
$$101x = 505$$
$$x = 5$$

   The number of minutes Charles spent studying for the final was 5 minutes.

THE CORRECT ANSWER IS 5.

NUMBERS

You should know all the basics about numbers, such as:

- Integers, fractions, rational, and real numbers

- Positive and negative:

    Zero (0) is neither positive nor negative.

- Even and odd

- Consecutive integers

- Fractions: common denominators:

$$\frac{a}{b} + \frac{c}{d} = \left(\frac{d}{d}\right)\frac{a}{b} + \left(\frac{b}{b}\right)\frac{c}{d} = \frac{ad + bc}{bd}$$

    For example:

$$\frac{1}{2} + \frac{1}{3} = \left(\frac{3}{3}\right)\frac{1}{2} + \left(\frac{2}{2}\right)\frac{1}{3} = \frac{5}{6}$$

- Fractions: cross-multiplication of equations:

    If $\frac{a}{b} = \frac{c}{d}$ then $ad = bc$

- Fractions: complex fractions:

$$\frac{\frac{a}{b}}{\frac{c}{d}} = \frac{a}{b} \times \frac{d}{c} = \frac{ad}{bc}$$

    For example:

$$\frac{\frac{1}{2}}{\frac{1}{3}} = \frac{1}{2} \times \frac{3}{1} = \frac{3}{2}$$

- Factors:

    For example:

    $$12 = 2 \times 2 \times 3$$

    The factors of 12 are 1, 2, 3, 4, 6, and 12.

- Prime numbers:

    A prime number has only two factors—1 and itself.

- Greatest common factor:

    For example:

    The greatest common factor of 8 and 12 is 4.

- Least common multiple:

    For example:

    The least common multiple of 8 and 12 is 24.

- Ratios:

    For example:

    If there are 7 spam e-mails for every 2 desired ones, the ratio of spam e-mails to desired e-mails can be written in the following equivalent ways:

    7 to 2   7:2 $\dfrac{7}{2}$

6.

Let p equal the number of times Olga has to shave her mustache today. If p is odd, which of the following is also odd?

(A) $2p + 2$
(B) $3p + 3$
(C) $p^2 + 1$
(D) $p^3 - 1$
(E) $p^4 + p + 1$

SOLUTION: The general rules for addition and multiplication for odd and even numbers are:

odd + odd = even	odd × odd = odd
even + even = even	even × even = even
odd + even = odd	odd × even = even

Apply these rules to the answer choices, and remember that $p^2 = p \cdot p$, $p^3 = p \cdot p \cdot p$, and $p^4 = p \cdot p \cdot p \cdot p$, and you'll find that only (E) is odd. For example, consider the term $2p + 2$ in (A). The $2p$ term is even times odd, which is even. Therefore, $2p + 2$ is even plus even, which is even.

THE CORRECT ANSWER IS (E).

ANOTHER APPROACH

The Plugging In Numbers method can save a lot of time on this question. The answer should hold true no matter what number p is (as long as it's odd), so let's let $p = 1$. If we plug in $p = 1$ to all the answer choices, only (E) gives us an odd answer.

7. The ratio of the number of Jessica's zits to the number of Serena's zits is 3:2. If Jessica has 24 zits, how many zits does Serena have?

SOLUTION:

$$\frac{\text{number of Jessica's zits}}{\text{number of Serena's zits}} = \frac{3}{2}$$

Jessica has 24 zits, so

$$\frac{24}{\text{number of Serena's zits}} = \frac{3}{2}$$

Cross-multiply to obtain the equation

$$(24)(2) = (3)(\text{number of Serena's zits})$$

Therefore, Serena has $\frac{48}{3} = 16$ zits.
THE CORRECT ANSWER IS 16.

WORD OF ADVICE
Take the few seconds it takes to double-check your answer. Plugging in 16 for the number of Serena's zits, we get a ratio of 24:16, which is the same as 3:2, so we're good.

8. On a scale of 1 to 10, Warren's hotness can be expressed as $a\sqrt{b}$, where a and b are positive integers and $a \geq b$. If Warren's hotness is equal to $2\sqrt{12}$, what is the value of $a - b$?
   (A) −10
   (B) −1
   (C) 0
   (D) 1
   (E) 10

SOLUTION: Your first thought might be to set $a = 2$ and $b = 12$, but that would be incorrect because we need a to be greater than or equal to b. Therefore, we need to find an equivalent way to write $2\sqrt{12}$.

$$2\sqrt{12} = 2\sqrt{4 \times 3} = 2(\sqrt{4})(\sqrt{3}) = 2(2)(\sqrt{3}) = 4\sqrt{3}$$

Therefore, $a = 4$ and $b = 3$. Therefore, $a - b = 1$.
THE CORRECT ANSWER IS (D).

NUMBERS—CONSECUTIVE INTEGERS

Consecutive integers differ by one, so if two numbers are consecutive they can be written as x and $x + 1$ (where x is the smaller of the two) or $x - 1$ and x (where x is the bigger of the two). For example:

---

9. R. Kelly parties with 5 girls whose ages are given by consecutive integers. The total age of the 5 girls is 75. What is the age of the oldest girl?
   (A) 13
   (B) 14
   (C) 15
   (D) 16
   (E) 17

SOLUTION: Let x equal the age of the oldest girl. The ages of the girls are consecutive integers, so that means their ages (in decreasing order) are $x, x - 1, x - 2, x - 3$, and $x - 4$. Therefore,

$$\begin{aligned} x + (x - 1) + (x - 2) + (x - 3) + (x - 4) &= 75 \\ 5x - 10 &= 75 \\ 5x &= 85 \\ x &= 17 \end{aligned}$$

THE CORRECT ANSWER IS (E).

CAREFUL!

A common error made by students is not setting x equal to the thing asked for in the question. For example, if you let x equal the age of the youngest girl, you obtain the equation:

$$x + (x + 1) + (x + 2) + (x + 3) + (x + 4) = 75$$

which leads to $x = 13$. Thirteen is indeed the age of the youngest girl, so as long as you remember to add 4, you could still get the right answer. However, quite often if you're in a rush, you'll forget to add the 4 at the end. That's why it's smart to let x equal the thing asked for in the question, which in this case is the age of the oldest girl.

ANOTHER APPROACH

You can also use the Plugging In Answers method for this question.

WORD OF ADVICE

Take the few seconds it takes to double-check your answer. Plugging in 17 for the age of the oldest girl, we get 17 + 16 + 15 + 14 + 13, which does equal 75, so we're good.

NUMBER LINES

You should know how to read number lines. For example:

10.

Lindsay Lohan measures out the above number line with a razor blade. What is the value of Q?

SOLUTION: The two points we know are 0.24 and 0.25, so the total distance between them is

$$\text{Total Distance} = 0.25 - 0.24 = 0.01$$

There are 8 more ruler marks to get from 0.24 to 0.25, so that means each ruler mark is $\frac{1}{8}$th of the total distance between the two points. In other words, the first mark after 0.24 is given by:

$$\text{First Mark} = 0.24 + \frac{1}{8}(0.01) = 0.24125$$

Similarly, the second mark is given by:

$$\text{Second Mark} = 0.24 + \frac{2}{8}(0.01) = 0.2425$$

And so on. Q is given by the fifth mark after 0.24, so its value is:

$$Q = 0.24 + \frac{5}{8}(0.01) = 0.24625$$

On a grid-in question would be filled in as .246.
THE CORRECT ANSWER IS 0.246.

CAREFUL!
A common error that some students make is to count the starting ruler mark for 0.24, count up 9 ruler marks total, and then work in terms of $\frac{1}{9}$th instead of $\frac{1}{8}$th. However, the starting point, 0.24 in this case, is like the 0 point, so it doesn't count. If it helps, you can mark up the number line and write $\frac{1}{8}$th, $\frac{2}{8}$th, $\frac{3}{8}$th, and so on, and if you did it right then you'll reach $\frac{8}{8}$th when you hit the end point of 0.25.

PERCENT

You should know how to work with percentages. In particular:

- Finding a percentage of a number:

$$X\% \text{ of } Y = (\frac{X}{100})Y$$

- Finding a percentage change:

$$\text{Percentage Change} = 100 \times \frac{\text{New Value} - \text{Original Value}}{\text{Original Value}}$$

- Finding a new value:

$$\text{New Value} = (1 + \frac{\text{Percentage Change}}{100}) \text{ Original Value}$$

For example:

A number increased by 8% = 1.08 × number

A number decreased by 8% = 0.92 × number

---

11. Rock group Blue Oyster Cult starts off with a cowbell level of 68. Legendary music producer Bruce Dickinson asks them to give him 50 percent more cowbell. What cowbell level does legendary music producer Bruce Dickinson want from Blue Oyster Cult?
    (A) 34
    (B) 71.4
    (C) 102
    (D) 340
    (E) 3,400

SOLUTION: Legendary music producer Bruce Dickinson is asking for a cowbell level of:

$$(1 + \frac{50}{100})68 = (1.5)68 = 102$$

THE CORRECT ANSWER IS (C).

12. Star Jones loses 160 pounds on the gastric bypass surgery diet. If her original weight was 300 pounds, how much weight (expressed as a percentage) did Star Jones lose on the gastric bypass surgery diet?

SOLUTION:

$$\text{Percentage Change} = 100 \times \frac{300 - 160}{300}$$

$$= 46.\overline{6}$$

Star Jones lost $46.\overline{6}\%$ of her weight on the gastric bypass surgery diet. On a grid-in question, this number is filled in as 46.7 (or 46.6 would also be counted as correct). THE CORRECT ANSWER IS 46.7 (OR 46.6).

CAREFUL!
Don't forget to divide by 100 or multiply by 100 when dealing with percentages.

ABSOLUTE VALUE

You should know how to work with absolute values. In particular:

- If $a > 0$ then $|a| = a$

  For example: $|2| = 2$

- If $a < 0$ then $|a| = -a$

  For example: $|-2| = 2$

- The absolute value of a number is always greater than or equal to zero.

- If $|x| = c$ then either $x = c$ or $-x = c$

- If $|x + b| < c$ then either $x + b < c$ or $-(x + b) < c$

- If $|x + b| > c$ then either $x + b > c$ or $-(x + b) > c$

---

13. Sean gives Joel one wedgie, three Indian burns, two purple nurples, and x swirlies as punishment for narcing on him to the teacher.

    If x is an even integer, and $|x - 6| < 3$, what is a possible value for x?

SOLUTION:
Either

$$x - 6 < 3$$
$$x < 9$$

or,

$$-(x - 6) < 3$$
$$-x < -3$$
$$x > 3$$

Therefore, $3 < x < 9$. But x is an even integer, so x is either 4, 6, or 8.

Notice that there are multiple correct answers for this grid-in question. We can choose any one of 4, 6, or 8 and get the answer right.

THE CORRECT ANSWER IS 4, 6, OR 8.

CAREFUL!

A very common error is to forget to reverse inequality signs when dividing by −1.

ANOTHER APPROACH

You can use the Plugging In Numbers approach for this question as well. An obvious choice for x is 6, because 6 is even, and $|6 - 6| = 0$, which is indeed less than 3.

EXPONENTS

You should know how to work with exponents, including:

- The rules of exponents:

$$x^0 = 1$$

$$x^{-m} = \frac{1}{x^m}$$

$$x^{\frac{m}{n}} = \sqrt[n]{x^m}$$

$$x^m \cdot x^n = x^{m+n}$$

$$\frac{x^m}{x^n} = x^{m-n}$$

$$(x^m)^n = x^{mn}$$

- For an equation involving exponents, try getting it into a common base.

- If $x^2 = 4$, then $x = 2$ or $x = -2$. If $\sqrt{x} = 4$, then $x = 16$ (and not -16).

---

14. Ninety-nine bottles of beer are on the wall. If b bottles of beer are taken down and passed around, where b is the solution to the equation $(2^{b-1})^4 = 8^{b+2}$, how many bottles of beer remain on the wall?

SOLUTION: Let's get the equation into a common base so we can compare exponents.

$$\text{Left side: } (2^{b-1})^4 = 2^{4b-4} \qquad \text{Right side: } 8^{b+2} = (2^3)^{b+2} = 2^{3b+6}$$

So if $2^{4b-4} = 2^{3b+6}$ then it must mean that the exponents are equal to each other. Therefore:

$$4b - 4 = 3b + 6$$
$$b = 10$$

There are 10 bottles of beer that were taken down and passed around. Therefore the number of bottles of beer that remain on the wall is $99 - 10 = 89$.
THE CORRECT ANSWER IS 89.

NUMBERS BETWEEN 0 AND 1

We normally think that multiplying by a number makes it bigger and dividing by a number makes it smaller, but that isn't true for numbers between 0 and 1. For example, dividing a number by a half is actually the same as doubling that number. So be careful when you're asked to make general statements about numbers to always consider numbers between 0 and 1 as well. For example:

---

15. Let x represent the percentage of time Larry thinks about sex (whether he admits it or not). Let $p = 100 - x$.

    If $0 < p < 1$, which of the following represents the correct ordering of $\sqrt{p}$, p, and p^2?

    (A) $\sqrt{p} < p < p^2$
    (B) $\sqrt{p} < p^2 < p$
    (C) $p < \sqrt{p} < p^2$
    (D) $p^2 < p < \sqrt{p}$
    (E) $p^2 < \sqrt{p} < p$

SOLUTION: We normally think of squaring a number as making it bigger and taking the square root as making it smaller, but that isn't true for numbers between 0 and 1. For $0 < p < 1$, squaring makes p smaller, while taking the square root makes p bigger. For example, if $p = \frac{1}{4}$, then $p^2 = \frac{1}{16}$ and $\sqrt{p} = \frac{1}{2}$.

THE CORRECT ANSWER IS (D).

COUNTING AND PROBABILITY

You should know the basics about counting problems and probability, including:

- The Fundamental Counting Principle:
    For two independent events, if there are m ways for the first event to occur, and n ways for the second event to occur, then there are $m \times n$ ways for both events to occur.

- Permutations and combinations:
    Permutations involve the number of ways to arrange items where the ordering of the items matter. Combinations involve the number of ways to choose items where the ordering of the items doesn't matter.

- The basic definition of probability:

$$\text{The probability of an event} = \frac{\text{the number of ways the event can happen}}{\text{the total number of ways things can happen}}$$

- The probability of something is always between 0 (it can never happen) and 1 (it will always happen).

---

16. A ninja can kill you 8 different ways using his hands, 3 different ways using his feet, and 2 different ways just by looking at you. How many different ways can the ninja kill 3 people if he kills 1 with his hands, 1 with his feet, and 1 by eye contact?
    (A) 13
    (B) 18
    (C) 24
    (D) 40
    (E) 48

SOLUTION:
    Number of ways to kill first person (by hand) = 8
    Number of ways to kill second person (by feet) = 3
    Number of ways to kill third person (by eyes) = 2
    These are three independent events, therefore the total number of ways to kill the three people equals the multiplication of the ways to kill each individual person. In other words,
    Number of ways to kill all three people = 8 × 3 × 2 = 48.
THE CORRECT ANSWER IS (E).

17. Two more spots must be filled on a baseball team, but the only 4 people remaining to choose from are the following spazzes: Norbert, Gilbert, Eugene, and Clifford. How many different pairs of spazzes can be chosen?

SOLUTION:

There are 4 ways to pick the first spaz.

There are 3 ways to pick the second spaz (because you can't pick the same spaz twice).

However, there are 2 equivalent orders in which the two spazzes can be chosen (because, for example, choosing Clifford first and Eugene second is the same as choosing Eugene first and Clifford second).

Therefore, the number of different pairs is 4 × 3 / 2 = 6.

The six pairs are: Norbert and Gilbert, Norbert and Eugene, Norbert and Clifford, Gilbert and Eugene, Gilbert and Clifford, and Eugene and Clifford.
THE CORRECT ANSWER IS 6.

ADVANCED FORMULAE

The general permutation and combination formulae (for those who wish to remember them) are as follows:

The number of ways to arrange m items from a collection of n things, where the ordering of the items matter, is:

$$P(n, m) = \frac{n!}{(n-m)!} = n \times (n-1) \times \ldots \times (n-m+1)$$

The number of ways to choose m items from a collection of n things, where the ordering of the items doesn't matter, is:

$$C(n, m) = \frac{n!}{(n-m)!\, m!} = \frac{n \times (n-1) \ldots \times (n-m+1)}{m \times (m-1) \times \ldots \times 1}$$

COUNTING AND PROBABILITY—FIRST PRINCIPLES

It's useful to know formulae, but sometimes the test makers want to make sure you understand the basic concepts, so they'll ask you a question where the formula doesn't directly apply. If you're ever stuck, don't be afraid to just count out all the possible arrangements in a brute force way. For example:

---

18. Uma Thurman, Drew Barrymore, Angelina Jolie, and Jennifer Aniston are to be seated in a row of 4 chairs. Angelina Jolie and Jennifer Aniston MUST NOT be seated next to each other. How many different such seating arrangements are possible?

SOLUTION: If we didn't have to care about who sat next to whom, we'd know how to solve this question. There would be 4 ways for the first seat, times 3 for the second seat, times 2 for the third seat, times 1 for the last seat, for a total of 24. But if Angelina Jolie and Jennifer Aniston can't sit next to each other, then how do we solve this problem? What's the formula?

The point is, if you're stuck, don't get bogged down on the formula. Use brute force and make a list of all the possible arrangements. Let's use U for Uma, D for Drew, A for Angelina, and J for Jennifer, and let's make a list. Let's also be consistent about it, so for example let's go through all the possible cases with A in the first spot, then all the cases with A in the second spot, and so on.

Our list is as follows:

$A D J U$
$A D U J$
$A U D J$
$A U J D$
$D A U J$
$U A D J$
$J D A U$
$J U A D$
$D J U A$
$J D U A$
$J U D A$
$U J D A$

THE CORRECT ANSWER IS 12.

Now let's consider how the same idea can come up in a probability question. For example:

---

19. If Uma Thurman, Drew Barrymore, Angelina Jolie, and Jennifer Aniston are seated randomly in a row of 4 chairs, what is the probability that Angelina Jolie and Jennifer Aniston will NOT be seated next to each other?

SOLUTION: Remember the basic idea behind probability:

$$\text{The probability of an event} = \frac{\text{the number of ways the event can happen}}{\text{the total number of ways things can happen}}$$

We used brute force in the previous problem to count that the number of ways Angelina Jolie and Jennifer Aniston are NOT seated next to each other is 12. We also know the total number of ways people can be seated (if we didn't care about constraints of who can't sit next to whom) is 24. Therefore the probability that Angelina Jolie and Jennifer Aniston are NOT seated next to each other is $\frac{12}{24}$, which equals $\frac{1}{2}$.

THE CORRECT ANSWER IS $\frac{1}{2}$ OR .5.

TO RECAP

It's important to know the mathematical formulae, but if you're ever stuck on a question, don't be afraid (or ashamed) to use brute force and just list out all the arrangements. Be systematic so you don't miss anything on the list.

DATA ANALYSIS AND ELEMENTARY STATISTICS

You should know a number of things, including:

- How to read tables, bar graphs, line graphs, pie charts, pictographs, and scatterplots

- Average (arithmetic mean) = $\dfrac{\text{sum of the numbers}}{\text{the number of items in the list}}$

- Median = the middle value (or average of the two middle values if there are an even number of items in the list)

- Mode = the number or set of numbers that appears the most

---

20. If the IQs of contestants on the reality show *A Shot at Love with Tila Taquila* are 60, 50, 80, 60, 70, 75, 40, and 90, what is the relationship between the average (arithmetic mean), median, and mode of the contestant IQs?
    (A) mode < median < mean
    (B) mode < mean < median
    (C) mean < median < mode
    (D) mean < mode < median
    (E) median < mode < mean

SOLUTION: Let's put the numbers in order:
$$40\ 50\ 60\ 60\ 70\ 75\ 80\ 90$$
Now we can calculate:
$$\text{mean} = (40 + 50 + 60 + 60 + 70 + 75 + 80 + 90) / 8 = 65.625$$
$$\text{median} = (60 + 70) / 2 = 65$$
$$\text{mode} = 60$$
which means that mode < median < mean.
THE CORRECT ANSWER IS (A).

21. Let x, y, and z equal the number of times Veronica, Ben, and Debbie respectively want to punch Terry in the face because he uses "LOL" in actual conversation instead of just in text messages and e-mails.

If the average (arithmetic mean) of x and y is 4, and the average of x, y, and z is 10, what is the value of z?

SOLUTION: Let's plug into the definition for finding an average. We are given two averages, so we get two equations:

$$\frac{x+y}{2} = 4 \quad \text{and} \quad \frac{x+y+z}{3} = 10$$

The first equation can be rewritten as $x + y = 8$. Now plug that in to the second equation to get

$$\frac{8+z}{3} = 10$$

Therefore,

$$z = (3)(10) - 8 = 22$$

THE CORRECT ANSWER IS 22.

STRAIGHT LINES

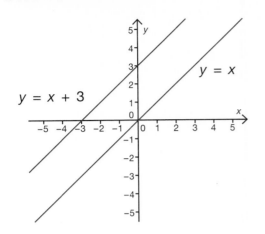
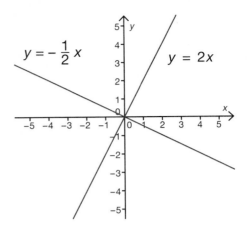

You should know all about straight lines in the xy-coordinate plane, including things like:

- The general equation for a straight line is:

$$y = mx + b$$

where m is the slope and b is the y-intercept.

- The y-intercept occurs when $x = 0$.

- On a graph, lines with positive slope get bigger as you move from left to right, while lines with negative slope get smaller.

- If two points on the line are (x_1, y_1) and (x_2, y_2), the slope is equal to the rise over the run, which is the amount that y changes divided by the amount that x changes. In other words:

$$\text{slope} = \frac{y_2 - y_1}{x_2 - x_1}$$

- Parallel lines have the same slope m.

- Perpendicular lines have slope $-1/m$.

- The distance, d, between any two points (x_1, y_1) and (x_2, y_2) is:

$$d = \sqrt{(x_2 - x_1)^2 + (y_2 - y_1)^2}$$

22.

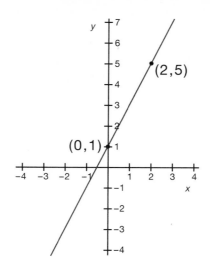

Tristan is at his girlfriend's apartment when she informs him that he's going to be a daddy. Tristan runs as far as he can along the straight line path depicted in the figure above. Which of the following is an accurate mathematical description for the straight line depicted in the figure above?

(A) $y = -2x + 1$

(B) $y = \frac{1}{2}x + 1$

(C) $y = x$

(D) $y = 2x + 1$

(E) $y = 3x + 1$

SOLUTION: When $x = 0$, $y = 1$, so the y-intercept, b, equals 1.

The slope can be found from the two points depicted on the line.

$$\text{slope } m = \frac{5-1}{2-0} = 2$$

Therefore the straight line can be expressed as $y = 2x + 1$.
THE CORRECT ANSWER IS (D).

23. Mob hitmen, Vincent and Jules, whack a snitch. In the *xy*-coordinate plane, Vincent's bullet travels a straight line with slope $\frac{1}{2}$ and passes through the point (4, 1). Jules's bullet travels in a perpendicular straight line passing through the origin. At what point in the plane do the two lines intersect?

(A) $\left(-\frac{4}{3}, \frac{2}{3}\right)$

(B) $\left(-\frac{4}{5}, \frac{2}{5}\right)$

(C) $\left(-\frac{1}{4}, -1\right)$

(D) $\left(\frac{2}{5}, -\frac{4}{5}\right)$

(E) $\left(\frac{2}{3}, -\frac{4}{3}\right)$

SOLUTION:

Vincent's bullet:

The slope is $\frac{1}{2}$, so the equation is:

$$y = \frac{1}{2}x + b$$

It also passes through the point (4, 1) so,

$$1 = \frac{1}{2}(4) + b$$

$$b = -1$$

Therefore, the equation for Vincent's bullet is:

$$y = \frac{1}{2}x - 1$$

Jules's bullet:

Jules's bullet makes a perpendicular line to Vincent's, so it has a slope of $\dfrac{-1}{\frac{1}{2}} = -2$.

Also, it passes through the origin, so the y-intercept is zero. The line is therefore given by the equation:

$$y = -2x$$

To find the point of intersection of the two lines, set the two equations equal to each other.

$$\frac{1}{2}x - 1 = -2x$$

$$\frac{5}{2}x = 1$$

$$x = \frac{2}{5}$$

Therefore,

$$y = -2\left(\frac{2}{5}\right) = -\frac{4}{5}$$

The two lines intersect at $\left(\frac{2}{5}, -\frac{4}{5}\right)$.

THE CORRECT ANSWER IS (D).

DIRECTLY OR INVERSELY PROPORTIONAL

Two variables x and y are said to be directly proportional or inversely proportional if:

Directly Proportional

$$y = kx \text{ for some positive constant } k$$

So if x *increases* by a factor of something, then y *increases* by the same factor.

Inversely Proportional

$$y = \frac{k}{x} \text{ for some positive constant } k$$

So if x *increases* by a factor of something, then y *decreases* by the same factor.

---

24. The time it takes for the LAPD to subdue a wrongly identified minority suspect is inversely proportional to the number of LAPD officers on the scene. If it takes a single LAPD officer 5 minutes to subdue a wrongly identified minority suspect, how many LAPD officers would it take to subdue a wrongly identified minority suspect in only 1 minute?

(A) $\frac{1}{5}$

(B) 1

(C) 5

(D) 25

(E) 50

SOLUTION: You could write $y = \frac{k}{x}$ and plug in numbers to find k, but a much faster way to go about it is to remember that, for inversely proportional, if x *decreases* by a factor of 5 then y *increases* by a factor of 5. So for the time to subdue a wrongly identified minority suspect to decrease by a factor of 5, the number of LAPD officers would have to increase by a factor of 5 as well, from a single LAPD officer to 5 LAPD officers.
THE CORRECT ANSWER IS (C).

PARABOLAS

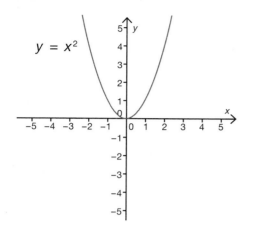

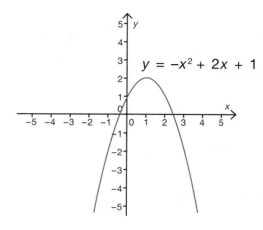

You should know some basics about parabolas, such as:

- The general equation is:

$$y = ax^2 + bx + c$$

- If $a > 0$ the parabola opens upward

  If $a < 0$ the parabola opens downward

- The y-intercept (which occurs when $x = 0$) is c

Although questions about parabolas look like they can get real messy (and they can), sometimes the questions are actually much simpler than they look. For example:

25. Taking care of vital national security issues, the President hits a golf ball whose height-distance relationship satisfies the equation $y = ax^2 + bx + c$ for $0 \leq x$ and $0 \leq y$.

   If $a < 0$ and $c = 0$, which of the following graphs could represent (for $0 \leq x$ and $0 \leq y$) the path of the golf ball?

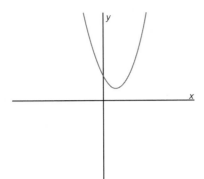

(A)

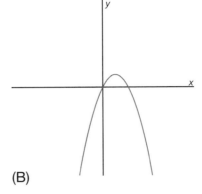

(B)

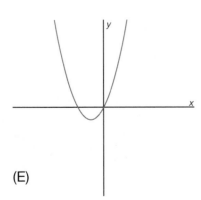

(C)

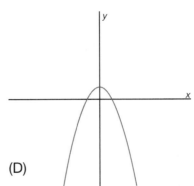

(D)

(E)

SOLUTION: If $a < 0$, then we know that the parabola opens downward, so we can eliminate choices (A) and (E). If $c = 0$, then we know that the y-intercept is zero, so we can eliminate choices (C) and (D).

THE CORRECT ANSWER IS (B).

FUNCTIONS

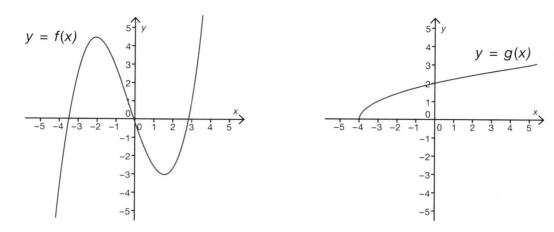

You should understand functions and function notation. Including:

- $f(x)$ (or g or h or whatever letter they use) is like the y-value in the xy-coordinate plane. In other words, for any value of x, the function f tells us the corresponding value of y, given as $y = f(x)$. Note that $f(x)$ is read as "f of x" and does not mean "f multiplied by x."

- domain = all the x-values where the function is defined

- range = all the y-values that the function can take

- $f(x + 1)$ is the same as $f(x)$ shifted left by 1,
  $f(x - 1)$ is the same as $f(x)$ shifted right by 1,
  $f(x) + 1$ is the same as $f(x)$ shifted up by 1, and
  $f(x) - 1$ is the same as $f(x)$ shifted down by 1.

---

26. Let the amount of profit a scalper makes from Hannah Montana tickets be given by the function, $P(x) = 437x - 12$, where x is the number of tickets sold by the scalper to an outraged mob of parents. If the scalper makes a profit of $8,728, how many Hannah Montana tickets did he sell?

SOLUTION: The profit is given to us as 8,728, so simply set $P(x)$ equal to 8,728 and solve for x.

$$8728 = P(x) = 437x - 12$$

$$x = \frac{8728 + 12}{437} = 20$$

THE CORRECT ANSWER IS 20 TICKETS.

27.

$g(x)$

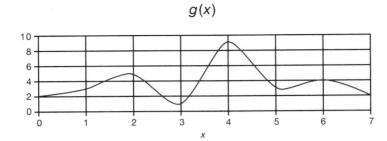

The degree to which Hector acts like a douchebag is ranked over time on a scale of 0 to 10. Hector's douchebag-level is mapped over the course of a week to create the function g, which is graphed in the figure. Approximately how much is $g(2)$?
(A) 2
(B) 3
(C) 4
(D) 5
(E) 5.5

SOLUTION: Remember, $g(2)$ is like the y-value when $x = 2$. When $x = 2$, the graph looks like it passes halfway between 4 and 6, therefore $g(2) = 5$.
THE CORRECT ANSWER IS (D).

FUNCTIONS—$g(f(x))$

You should understand the idea of a composition of functions. The composition of two functions, $g(f(x))$, means:

    1. First find $f(x)$.

    2. Treat $f(x)$ like the new x-value for the function g.

This sounds a lot harder than it actually is. For example:

---

28. The degree to which Hector acts like a douchebag is ranked over time on a scale of 0 to 10. Hector's douchebag-level is mapped over the course of a week to create the function g, which is graphed in the figure on page 98. Approximately how much is $g(g(2))$?

    (A) 3

    (B) 3.5

    (C) 4.75

    (D) 5

    (E) 5.5

SOLUTION:

    1. As we solved in the previous question, $g(2) = 5$.

    2. Now treat 5 as the new x-value. When $x = 5$, the graph looks like it passes halfway between 2 and 4, therefore $g(g(2)) = g(5) = 3$.

THE CORRECT ANSWER IS (A).

---

29. Suppose the return on investment for investing x dollars in Kevin Federline's career is given by the function, $f(x) = \frac{x}{10}$, and the return on investment for investing x dollars in Justin Timberlake's career is given by the function, $g(x) = x^2$.

If $p > 0$, what is the value of $g(f(p + 1))$?

    (A) $p^2 + \frac{p}{5} + \frac{1}{100}$

    (B) $p^2 + 2p + 1$

    (C) $\frac{p^2}{100} + \frac{p}{50} + \frac{1}{100}$

    (D) $\frac{p^2}{100} + 1$

    (E) $\frac{p^2}{100} + \frac{p}{50} + 1$

SOLUTION: Remember that what's inside the brackets of a function is like the x-value. Also remember what the notation means. $g(f(p+1))$ means to do the following:

1. Treat $(p+1)$ like the x-value in $f(x)$. That gives you $f(p+1)$.
2. Now treat $f(p+1)$ like the x-value in $g(x)$. That gives you $g(f(p+1))$.

Let's do it:

1. $$f(p+1) = \frac{p+1}{10}$$

2. $$g(f(p+1)) = g\left(\frac{p+1}{10}\right)$$

$$= \left(\frac{p+1}{10}\right)^2$$

$$= \frac{p^2 + 2p + 1}{100}$$

$$= \frac{p^2}{100} + \frac{p}{50} + \frac{1}{100}$$

THE CORRECT ANSWER IS (C).

CAREFUL!

A common error is to mix up the order of operations. Add extra brackets if it helps.

ANOTHER APPROACH

The Plugging In Numbers approach for this question can speed things up. Pick a number for p—let's say $p = 1$. Then $f(p+1) = f(2) = \frac{2}{10} = \frac{1}{5}$. Therefore $g(f(p+1)) = g\left(\frac{1}{5}\right) = \left(\frac{1}{5}\right)^2 = \frac{1}{25}$. If we plug $p = 1$ into all the answer choices, (C) is the only answer choice that equals $\frac{1}{25}$.

MADE-UP SYMBOLS

The made-up symbol question is a question where they give you a weird-looking symbol that you've never seen before and then they ask you to solve something involving that symbol. These questions may look really scary, but they're almost always much easier than they look, so don't get frightened off. Basically, they give you some instructions as to what the symbol means, and all you have to do is follow the instructions. For example:

---

30. A 30-year-old guy who has never kissed a girl makes up the following mathematical symbol at a Star Trek convention.

Let 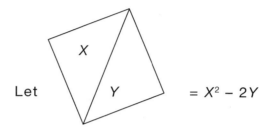 $= X^2 - 2Y$

for all integers X and Y. What is the value of

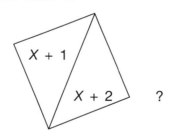 ?

(A) $X^2 - 3$
(B) $X^2 - 2X - 1$
(C) $X^2 - 2X - 3$
(D) $X^2 + 3$
(E) $X^2 - 1$

SOLUTION: Just follow the instructions. Treat $(X + 1)$ as the new X and treat $(X + 2)$ as the new Y.

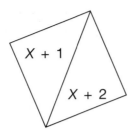

$$= (X + 1)^2 - 2(X + 2)$$
$$= X^2 + 2X + 1 - 2X - 4$$
$$= X^2 - 3$$

THE CORRECT ANSWER IS (A).

CAREFUL!
Some students get confused over the order of operations. Add extra brackets around the terms if you're confused and want to make sure you're doing the operations in the right order. For example, in this case, you don't square the X and then add 1. Instead, $(X + 1)$ is the new X and $(X + 2)$ is the new Y.

ANOTHER APPROACH
You can use the Plugging In Numbers approach for this question as well. Pick a number for X—let's say $X = -1$. Then by applying the weird symbol we get $0^2 - 2(1) = -2$. If we plug in $X = -1$ into the answer choices, only (A) gives us an answer of -2.

GEOMETRY

There are a ton of things to know about geometry. Things you should know include:

- Intersecting lines:

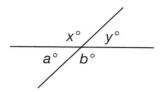

    Supplementary angles add up to 180°:

$$x + y = x + a = y + b = a + b = 180$$

    Vertical angles are equal:

$$x = b$$
$$y = a$$

- A line intersecting two parallel lines:

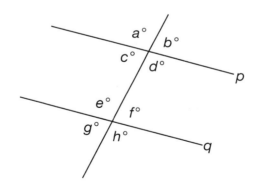

$$a = d = e = h$$
$$b = c = f = g$$

- Sum of the angles in a polygon:
    Sum of the angles in a triangle = 180°
    Sum of the angles in a quadrilateral = 360°
    Sum of the angles in a pentagon = 540°
    and so on (keep adding 180° for every new side)

- Area and perimeter:

  Area of a triangle = $\frac{1}{2}$ (base × height)

  Area of a rectangle = length × width

  Area of a square = side^2 (side = length = width)

  Perimeter = sum of the length of all the sides

- The Triangle Inequality:

  The length of the third side of a triangle is less than the sum of the lengths of the other two sides and greater than the difference of the lengths of the other two sides.

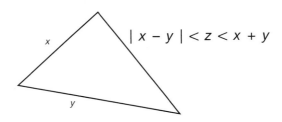

- Isosceles triangles:

  2 sides have equal length

  Corresponding angles are equal

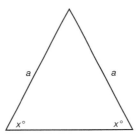

- Equilateral triangles:

  All 3 sides have equal length

  All angles are equal to 60°

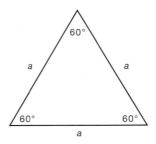

- Similar triangles:
    Corresponding angles are equal
    Corresponding sides have the same ratio

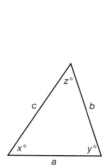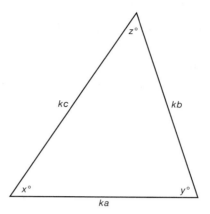

- Right triangles:
    Pythagorean Theorem: $a^2 + b^2 = c^2$

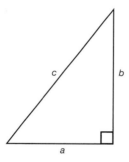

- 45-45-90 triangles:
    Sides are in the ratio of $1:1:\sqrt{2}$

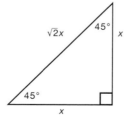

- 30-60-90 triangles:
  Sides are in the ratio of $1:\sqrt{3}:2$

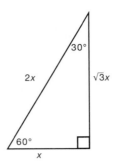

- Circles:

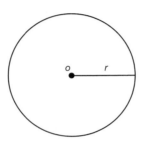

$$\text{radius} = r$$
$$\text{diameter} = 2r$$
$$\text{circumference} = 2\pi r$$
$$\text{area} = \pi r^2$$

- Volume and surface area:
  Volume of a cube = side^3
  Volume of a rectangular solid = length × width × height
  Volume of a right circular cylinder = $\pi r^2 h$
  Surface Area = sum of areas of all the faces

Whew! Now back to the funny questions.

31.

After Karen is dumped by Peter for that slut, Janine, Karen crosses out all pictures of Peter with a big black marker, drawing lines in a manner depicted in the figure above. If the 4 lines all intersect at the same point, and $y = 50$, what is the value of x?

(A) 25
(B) 35
(C) 40
(D) 45
(E) 50

SOLUTION: The portion between the 65 and the y is a vertical angle, which means it is also 25°. Let's now use the fact that the total angle of a straight line is 180° to obtain the equation,

$$x + 65 + 25 + y = 180$$

We were also told that $y = 50$, so that means,

$$x + 65 + 25 + 50 = 180$$

which we can solve as,

$$x = 40$$

THE CORRECT ANSWER IS (C).

32. Lindsay Lohan, Aaron Carter, and Hilary Duff form the vertices of a love triangle. If one side of the triangle has a measure of 5, a second side has a measure of 9, and the third side has a measure that is an even number, what is the minimum possible value for the perimeter of the love triangle?

SOLUTION: The Triangle Inequality states that the length of the third side is less than the sum of the lengths of the other two sides and greater than the difference of the lengths of the other two sides. Therefore:

$$9 - 5 < \text{length of third side} < 9 + 5$$

or, in other words,

$$4 < \text{length of third side} < 14$$

The third side is said to be an even number, so that means the length of the third side can be 6, 8, 10, or 12.

The perimeter is equal to the sum of the lengths of the three sides, so the smallest perimeter would occur when the length of the third side is 6.

The smallest perimeter $= 5 + 9 + 6 = 20$.

THE CORRECT ANSWER IS 20.

33.

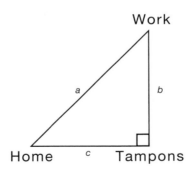

While at work, Bill is teased by his colleagues for being "whipped." After angrily denying the charges, Bill makes a pit stop at the drugstore on his way home in order to buy some tampons. In the figure, what is the relationship between the distances a, b, and c?

(A) $a^2 + b^2 = c^2$

(B) $a^2 + c^2 = b^2$

(C) $b^2 - c^2 = a^2$

(D) $c^2 - b^2 = a^2$

(E) $a^2 - b^2 = c^2$

SOLUTION: This is a right triangle, so the Pythagorean Theorem states that the square of the length of the hypotenuse equals the sum of the squares of the lengths of the other two sides. Therefore,

$$a^2 = b^2 + c^2$$

Now subtract b^2 from both sides to get

$$a^2 - b^2 = c^2$$

THE CORRECT ANSWER IS (E).

CAREFUL!
The Pythagorean Theorem is normally remembered by the equation $a^2 + b^2 = c^2$, but that's if c is the length of the hypotenuse. In our triangle, a is the length of the hypotenuse. Be careful on the test because there can be questions like this which test that you really understand the formula, and are not just memorizing an equation that you don't fully understand.

34.

In the figure, if $x = 5 - y$, what is the value of $y^2 + 25$?
(A) 7
(B) 32
(C) 39
(D) 56
(E) 64

SOLUTION: Don't get frightened by the x and y. This is a right triangle, so apply the Pythagorean Theorem and see what happens. We were told that $x = 5 - y$, so the Pythagorean Theorem gives us,

$$(5 - y)^2 + (y + 5)^2 = 8^2$$

Expand it out to get,

$$25 - 10y + y^2 + y^2 + 10y + 25 = 64$$

The $-10y$ and $10y$ cancel each other, so we are left with,

$$2(y^2 + 25) = 64$$

which means

$$y^2 + 25 = 32$$

THE CORRECT ANSWER IS (B).

GEOMETRY—ARC OF A CIRCLE

For questions involving arcs of a circle, remember that there are 360 degrees in a complete circle. Use that fact to figure out what portion of the total circle you are dealing with. For example:

35.

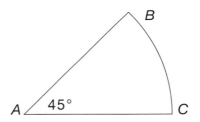

Before falling on her ass and losing the gold medal to the Russians, Sasha Cohen skates a perfect arc of a circle with center A. If the length of arc BC is 3π and the measure of $\angle BAC$ is 45°, what is the area of sector ABC?

(A) 8π
(B) 18π
(C) 24π
(D) 36π
(E) 108π

SOLUTION: Use the fact that there are 360 degrees in a complete circle. Our portion of the circle is 45 degrees, so the portion of the circle we have is $\frac{45}{360}$ of the total, or $\frac{1}{8}$th of the total circle. That means the arc BC is $\frac{1}{8}$th of the total circumference of the circle. Therefore,

$$3\pi = \frac{1}{8}\text{ (circumference)}$$

$$= \frac{1}{8}(2\pi r)$$

$3\pi = \frac{2\pi}{8} \rightarrow \frac{\pi}{4}r$

$3\pi \div \frac{\pi}{4} = 12 = r$

Solve for r to get

$$r = 12$$

Now we can calculate the area of the total circle and then take $\frac{1}{8}$th of it to get the area of sector ABC.

$$\text{Area of Circle} = \pi r^2 = \pi(12)^2 = 144\pi$$

$$\text{Area of Sector } ABC = \frac{1}{8}\text{ (Area of Circle)}$$

$$= \frac{1}{8}(144\pi)$$

$$= 18\pi$$

THE CORRECT ANSWER IS (B).

GEOMETRY—UNUSUAL SHAPES

For the unusual shape question, they give you a weird-looking shape and ask you a question about it. The question might look really hard at first, as if it involves math you've never heard of before, but it's really not that hard. The unusual shape is always made up of other shapes (or parts of shapes) that you know quite well. For example:

36.

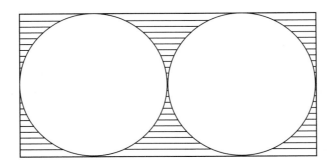

After a night of heavy drinking, Mike wakes up with no memory of the night before and with a tattoo on his butt in the shape of the figure shown. The diameter of each circle is 2 and the circles are tangent to each other and to the enclosing rectangle. What is the area of the shaded region of the figure?

(A) $2 - 2\pi$

(B) $8 - 2\pi$

(C) 8π

(D) $8 - 8\pi$

(E) $32 - 8\pi$

SOLUTION: In this case, the shaded part is simply the rectangle minus the two circles. So:

$$\text{Shaded Area} = \text{Area of Rectangle} - \text{Area of Circles}$$

The circles we know because they give us the diameter, but what about the rectangle? What is its length and width? Well, the circles help us out here as well. The circles are tangent to the rectangle and to each other, so the width of the rectangle is equal to the diameter of one circle and the length of the rectangle is equal to twice the diameter, which is the length of the two circles back to back. Therefore:

$$\text{Shaded Area} = (4)(2) - \pi(1)^2 - \pi(1)^2 = 8 - 2\pi$$

THE CORRECT ANSWER IS (B).

radius (diameter is 2)

WAYS TO IMPROVE YOUR SCORE

1. **Practice and Review**

   Do a ton of sample problems, starting with the Math practice sections we've provided. If you find you're weak in certain areas, go back and review those areas.

2. **Know the Techniques**

   Know the two techniques of Plugging In Answers and Plugging In Numbers and when to apply them.

3. **Don't Get Scared**

   As you've seen, oftentimes they'll give you questions that require you to think a little before you can apply well-known formulas. Don't be frightened by questions that at first look as if they have nothing to do with any math you've ever learned. Try to reason things out and don't be afraid to plug in different numbers to see if that leads to a better understanding. Remember, it's not only a math test, but a reasoning test as well.

4. **Check Your Work**

   The answer choices are designed with some of the most common student errors in mind, so it's quite possible you made a careless error somewhere along the way and didn't notice it because your answer was one of the answer choices. If you have the time, take a few moments to check your work for careless errors. It may even be worth skipping one really hard problem you're stuck on and using that time to check over all of your other answers.

   When you're checking your work, it's often useful to take a different approach and see if you still get the same answer. That's a great indication that you got the question right. For example, if you initially solved a question directly, try another approach such as the Plugging In Answers or Plugging In Numbers method when you check over your work.

Reality Check

Okay, so you probably won't get any math questions about Lindsay Lohan's drug problems on an actual SAT* exam. You will definitely, though, see very similar math questions, only not quite as funny. Now that you've gone through our review, you know all about the Math portion of the exam and how to solve many of the most common types of problems on the test. You've also learned two very powerful techniques to help you find the answer even if you don't fully understand how to solve the question.

The Math practice sections will give you a chance to practice what you've learned and will more fully test your knowledge of the areas of math you need to know for the exam. Feel free to jump to the Math practice sections beginning on page 159 at this point, or save them until after you've gone through the Critical Reading and Writing reviews as well.

PART 5
REALITY CHECK

Reality Check

Congratulations! You've made it through the review sections and now you know all about the different types of questions you'll get on the SAT* exam, and how to approach them. However, you might also be asking yourself, "Okay, some of those questions were pretty funny, but I won't see questions like this on the real exam—will I?"

It's true, in this book we use slang that you'll never see on an actual exam, but we use it in ways to teach proper English, and in all cases it is quite obvious what the slang is versus the areas of proper English being tested. Similarly, it's true that the math questions on the SAT* exam won't include questions about Brad and Angelina, Paris and Nicole, or any other celebrity or wannabe, but the actual math itself is *exactly* the type of question you'll find on the real exam.

So actually, you *will* find these types of questions on a real SAT* exam, with one main difference:

THE REAL EXAM IS **BORING!**

Instead of funny sentences, you'll get the dullest and most dry sentences ever to come out of an embalmed test maker's mouth.

Instead of funny passages, you'll get some monotonously boring passages about obscure art, history, science, and some dead guy's biography. Even if the subject is interesting, they'll somehow figure out how to give you the most boring passage ever written on the subject.

Instead of funny math problems, you'll just get . . . math problems.

Hopefully, an adrenaline rush will keep you going during the actual exam, but just in case, here are a few tips to stay awake and keep your focus during the test:

- If you find yourself starting to lose focus, pinch your nipples (or other appropriate body part) really hard until it hurts. [Note: Pinching other people's nipples is not allowed and totally inappropriate.]

- Wherever you see the word "builder" or "baker" in a math problem, try replacing it with the name of your favorite actor or actress, or baseball or basketball player.

- Take a few seconds to think about toe-jam. Nasty, smelly, slimy toe-jam. Or think about a dentist's drill. Or, if you're really desperate, think about your parents doing it, and they're into bondage. Now go back to the test. Suddenly, any boring passage or math problem will magically become *way* more interesting to think about.

- Make yourself a bet that you'll streak through your school if you don't achieve the minimum score you've set for yourself. Remind yourself of this bet whenever you find yourself losing steam during a section. Bear down and finish that section! Never give up! [Note: Do not attempt this technique if you are an exhibitionist.]

WHAT NOW?

If you haven't worked through the practice sections we've provided, do it now. They will help crystallize and expand on everything you've learned or reviewed so far. Work through the practice sections, laugh your butt off along the way, and then come back here. We'll wait . . .

DAH, DAH, DAH, DA DA DA DA DA, DA DA DA DA DA . . . DAH, DAH, DAH, DA DA DA DA DA, DA DA DA DA DA . . .

Oh, you're back! Hold on. Let me just pause my TiVo.

OK, now you're ready for the next phase of your SAT* exam preparation—taking actual exams. Yes, you actually need to work through some. In fact, people who score very high on the exam generally practice by taking between 5 and 10 full official tests. This is an extremely important part of the process and you would need to do this no matter which study guide you worked through, because you aren't graded on a study guide—you're graded on an actual exam. What we've hopefully done is taken the suckiest part of studying for the exam—the part that makes some people give up or not study in the first place—and made it suck a lot less. We've also given you all the tools you need to ace the actual test, but in a fun and memorable way that you should be able to recall better on test day. However, remember that the actual exam is dry and boring, so that's going to add another level of difficulty. That's how test makers get their kicks. Their lives suck, so they take it out on you.

After you've completed a full official test, you'll have a better sense of where you stand. For example, are you running out of time in the Critical Reading sections? It's very likely you'll find that the passages on the SAT* exam are a bit harder than ours, particularly because our passages are interesting and funny, so that's to be expected. However, if you're actually running out of time in the Critical Reading sections, then you need to start reading a lot more. Read whatever you want—newspapers, sci-fi, thrillers, bathroom stalls. Just read. Reading comprehension skills don't improve overnight. How about your vocabulary? Are there too many words that you don't understand? Then you should consider buying a vocabulary-builder book to slowly start building your vocabulary. Again, it doesn't happen overnight.

How are you doing with the Writing sections? Do you feel comfortable writing essays? If not, write more. Write essays in your e-mails and freak your friends out. Start a blog because you're the most important person in the universe and everyone needs to know what you ate for breakfast. Practice makes perfect. What about the sentence errors—are you catching most of them? If not, perhaps you're answering the questions too quickly. Some sentences are particularly complicated to try to trick you. However, the underlying sentence errors are ones that you've learned in this book. Keep them in mind at all times and look very closely for them.

Finally, what about the Math sections? Are you making a lot of careless errors? If so, then you need to force yourself to double-check your answers. Are there particular areas of math that are still giving you difficulty? Then you need to review those areas again or ask for help until you understand them. Also, have you been applying the Plugging In Answers and Plugging In Numbers methods when appropriate? You can save a lot of time if you know how to use these techniques, plus they provide another way of looking at questions when you're stuck, and a way to check your work to make sure you haven't fallen for one of the answer traps.

Your score on an actual, official exam should provide a good indication of where you stand and which areas you need to work on. Work on those areas to improve your score and then take another sample test and see how much you improve. Continue this process until you reach a score you're happy with. That's when you know you're ready for the real thing.

All right, that's about it. It's time to pull out an actual SAT* exam to see how far you've truly come. Good luck!

NOW GO KICK SOME SAT* ASS!

PART 6
PRACTICE TEST

Critical Reading Practice Section 1

24 QUESTIONS

TIME: 25 MINUTES

1. Peter felt _____ when he discovered Paula had cheated on him, so he posted nude photos of her on the Internet.
   (A) obliged
   (B) disheartened
   (C) betrayed
   (D) bemused
   (E) indifferent

2. Christopher questioned the _____ of his career aptitude test when the results _____ he should become a Pokémon Master.
   (A) subsistence, stipulated
   (B) beliefs, implied
   (C) efficacy, recommended
   (D) motivation, counseled
   (E) veracity, ruled

CONTINUE ON NEXT PAGE ➡

124

3. After a _____ investigation, the
inspector _____ that faulty wiring
was foshizzle the cause of the fire that
burned down Snoop Dogg's hizzouse.
(A) lengthy, realized
(B) complete, prognosticated
(C) cursory, ruled
(D) thorough, determined
(E) copious, charged

4. Paris could hardly think straight
because of the _____ racket and
because she wasn't all that bright.
(A) harmonious
(B) epigrammatic
(C) cerulean
(D) cacophonous
(E) immaterial

5. Tara was _____ to learn that her left
boob had popped out of her dress,
_____ her botched plastic surgery to
all the paparazzi.
(A) surprised, divulging
(B) mortified, exposing
(C) enthused, clarifying
(D) indisposed, secreting
(E) affronted, ascertaining

CONTINUE ON NEXT PAGE ➡

DIRECTIONS: The following passages are each followed by questions related to their content. Answer the questions based on what is <u>written</u> in the passage, and on what may be <u>implied</u> from the passage.

Wow. Read something and answer questions on it. Yeah, that was hard. Um . . . sorry I have to ask, but have you considered McDonalds? I hear they have openings . . .

Questions 6–7 are based on the following passage.

I love how they put animation in commercials to "prove their points." Does anyone actually say, "Oh my God, that
Line Pro-V conditioner is releasing little vitamin
5 droplets on her hair. That's amazing!"
Or, "Look, that man with the sunglasses. Those harmful UV ray arrows are bouncing off in the opposite direction, but the regular light arrows are getting through. I
10 have to get me a pair of those!" Or, "Wow, that detergent molecule is attaching itself to the dirt molecule. You know, I used to think this whole detergent thing was a total scam. But look, it really works!"

6. Which of the following would the author most likely add to the list of animation examples described in the passage?
(A) The Pillsbury Doughboy laughing when poked in the stomach.
(B) Tony the Tiger eating Frosted Flakes and exclaiming, "They're GGGGGGREAT!"
(C) Barney stealing Fred Flintstone's Fruity Pebbles.
(D) The Geico Gecko stating that you can save time and money on your car insurance.
(E) Lysol disinfectant spray killing cartoon germs.

7. Based on the passage, the author would most likely agree that
(A) people are gullible by nature
(B) a hand-drawn illustration of performance does not confirm the efficacy of a product
(C) animations are ineffective and should be banned from commercials
(D) people should turn off the TV and read more books
(E) animation is an effectual tool in the marketing of sunglasses

CONTINUE ON NEXT PAGE

Questions 8–9 are based on the following passage.

"You snooze, you die," says a new study in this month's issue of the journal *SLEEP*. According to a new study, apparently funded by Maxwell House, people who sleep the recommended eight hours a day actually have a higher death rate than people who sleep significantly fewer hours. When asked about his findings, the study's chief scientist said, "Must . . . stay . . . awake. Must . . . stay . . . awake. Huh? Wha? Who's there? Get your stinking paws off me, you damn dirty ape!" Ironically, the journal *SLEEP* is excellent bedtime reading.

8. The primary purpose of the passage is to
    (A) snidely criticize a policy decision
    (B) factually explain a scientific approach
    (C) humorously comment on a news story
    (D) wittily defend a health study
    (E) fictionally quote an authority

9. The state of mind of the study's chief scientist at the time of his quote can best be characterized as
    (A) altered
    (B) livid
    (C) lucid
    (D) logical
    (E) inebriated

Questions 10–14 are based on the following passage.

For decades, scientists have beamed messages into outer space in an attempt to contact alien civilizations. Now here's what I'd like to ask: What are they thinking? They're actually broadcasting the existence and location of our planet for the entire universe to see? As far as I'm concerned, that's treason. You might as well put up a giant neon space sign, saying, "Come invade us. Enslave our world." See, that's what happens when you take religion out of the classroom. Maybe all you left-wing radical nut-job scientists want to bow down to Zorlak, but leave me out of it. Listen in—I'm all for that—but don't transmit.

Now, I'll tell you what we're doing right. NASA's New Horizons Space Probe, launched last week, is now on its way to Pluto. That's good science. We'll conduct a little reconnaissance, check out their defenses, and then, when the time is right—Whammo! Right in the tentacles. Hey, we all know it's coming. It's either them or us. I'd rather it be them.

10. The author states a belief that war is imminent between
    (A) theists and atheists
    (B) Zorlak and theists
    (C) Earth and Pluto
    (D) NASA and left-wing radicals
    (E) Zorlak and left-wing radicals

CONTINUE ON NEXT PAGE ➡

11. In this passage, Zorlak most likely refers to
    (A) a scientist
    (B) an extraterrestrial
    (C) NASA
    (D) an alien warlord
    (E) Steven Spielberg

12. Based on the passage, the author would most like to see which of the following occur?
    (A) A repeal of the First Amendment rights to freedom of speech
    (B) An abandonment of science in favor of religion
    (C) A repeal of the separation of church and state, allowing religion to be taught in public schools
    (D) A total ban on the use of neon signs
    (E) Charges of treason brought against NASA

13. In this passage, the author advocates
    (A) a wait-and-see approach
    (B) attacking Pluto
    (C) the use of slavery
    (D) shutting down NASA
    (E) a live-and-let-live approach

14. An underlying assumption made by the author is that
    (A) humans are not alone in the universe
    (B) all scientists are left-wing radicals
    (C) science is sinful
    (D) NASA is an efficient government agency
    (E) extraterrestrials can understand Chinese

CONTINUE ON NEXT PAGE ➡

Questions 15–24 are based on the following passage.

Despite being threatened with sanctions and a referral to the U.N. Security Council, Iran continues to
Line blatantly defy America and the rest of the
5 world in its attempt to become a nuclear power. I, for one, would like to get MAD. No, I don't mean *angry*. I'm talking about M.A.D.—Mutually Assured Destruction. Okay, here's the thing. I just don't get
10 what the big deal is with letting these Iranians get nukes. I say, let them have them. Look, we've been through this all before—remember a little thing called the Cold War?
15 Here's how it works. First they build one warhead. Then we build two. Then they build ten. Then we build twenty. And so on, and so on, until we both have enough warheads to wipe out the planet
20 ten times over.

Scared? Don't be. The thing is they can't ever attack. They know that if they ever did, they'd be wiped off the map with our counter-response. And here's
25 the kicker: In the meantime, making them build all those missiles in the first place completely destroys their economy. I mean, each missile costs millions of dollars, right? Do the math. Pretty soon
30 those hummus lovers will be so bankrupt they'll be living in caves. Capitalism wins again, just as it did with the Russians.

Now sure, it may take thirty or forty years of living under the constant threat
35 of nuclear Armageddon for this process to play out, but there are upsides too. If you're a kid, playing games like Duck and Cover can be loads of fun. And what teenager hasn't used the pickup line,
40 "What if the world ended tomorrow?" to score them some make-out action, huh? I know I have. Plus, for the adults, well, there is simply no sweeter tasting cigarette than the one lit during an air raid siren.
45 So I say, bring on the nukes. Make them legal. The bad guys are just going to get them off the black market anyway. And after all, the right to bear arms is a cornerstone of our nation. If the NRA has
50 taught us anything, it's that the way to keep our citizens safe is not to try to keep weapons out of the hands of bad guys, but rather to make them freely available to anyone even on a moment's whim.
55 I'll go one step further—personal nukes for everyone. That's right. I have the right to protect myself with my own personal brand of atomic destruction. Think about it. What better way to keep your
60 neighbors honest. I'll bet that tightwad Higginbottoms would think twice about stealing my paper next time if he knew that not only would he die in a counter-strike, but so would his wife, his two bratty kids,
65 his pets, and half of New York City. So don't get mad, America, get M.A.D.

15. The primary purpose of the passage is to
   (A) refute a popular position
   (B) advocate a policy
   (C) expound on a strategy
   (D) analyze a course of action
   (E) support a point of view

CONTINUE ON NEXT PAGE ➡

16. Which of the following is the most likely place for this passage to be published?
    (A) An obscure entomology journal
    (B) The review section of the *LA Times* newspaper
    (C) A classified Pentagon memo
    (D) A best-selling political novel
    (E) The Op-Ed page of the *New York Times* newspaper

17. In line 6, "I, for one, would like to get MAD," reflects the author's
    (A) feelings of resentment toward Iran
    (B) desire for a policy shift concerning the problem of Iran obtaining nuclear capabilities
    (C) incomprehension of a climate of fear surrounding Iran
    (D) nihilistic tendencies
    (E) deep skepticism of the efficacy of the United Nations

18. The author's utilization of the Cold War (line 14), indicates an underlying view that
    (A) historians are wise
    (B) older people are wiser
    (C) lessons from the past can be applied to the present day
    (D) history always repeats itself
    (E) history often repeats itself

19. In line 30, "hummus lovers" is used as
    (A) an affectation
    (B) a reference to connoisseurs of middle eastern foods
    (C) a racial slight
    (D) a negative statement
    (E) a reference to someone in dire financial straits

20. The fourth paragraph (lines 33–44) primarily makes the argument that
    (A) there are positive aspects to living in constant fear of total annihilation
    (B) cigarettes can be pleasurable
    (C) if you play your cards right, you can score a kiss with a teenager
    (D) M.A.D. takes many years to play itself out
    (E) kids make the most of bad situations

21. In lines 60–65, Higginbottoms is portrayed as
    (A) an indigent suburbanite
    (B) a master thief
    (C) the author's environmentally conscious neighbor
    (D) penurious, too cheap to buy his own newspaper
    (E) an estimable figure

CONTINUE ON NEXT PAGE ➡

22. According to the author, if the policy of M.A.D. were in effect with respect to Iran, America would ultimately prevail because
    (A) Iran could no longer charge a high price for oil
    (B) Iran would be destroyed in a nuclear first strike
    (C) Iran would be destroyed in a nuclear counterattack
    (D) Iran's financial position would collapse
    (E) the United Nations would impose sanctions on Iran

23. The author would most likely support
    (A) a total ban on assault rifles
    (B) a three-day waiting period before a person can purchase a handgun
    (C) the abolition of the NRA
    (D) laws banning vigilantism
    (E) laws protecting gun manufacturers from lawsuits related to random shooting incidents

24. Which of the following statements could best serve to counter the author's arguments in support for the policy of M.A.D.?
    (A) During the Cold War, America was prosperous; currently America is in a recession.
    (B) During the Cold War, people were very patient; today people are anxious and in a hurry.
    (C) Statistics indicate that violent crimes have increased since the Cold War era.
    (D) The Cold-War Russians were logical; Iran is currently ruled by radical Mullahs.
    (E) Video game graphics have progressed far beyond the kind found in early games such as Duck and Cover.

S T O P
IF YOU FINISH BEFORE THE TIME ALLOTTED, YOU MAY
CHECK YOUR WORK IN *THIS SECTION ONLY*.

Critical Reading Practice Section 2

24 QUESTIONS

TIME: 25 MINUTES

DIRECTIONS: In the following sentences, each _____ indicates a word is missing. From among the five answer choices, choose the word, or set of words, that <u>best</u> fits the meaning of the sentence as a whole.

Uh, the directions didn't change since the last time, so why are you still reading these? Fill in the blanks!

1. Fran hired the _____ divorce attorney when she caught her husband shtupping his secretary.
   (A) passable
   (B) ruthless
   (C) lavish
   (D) cheapest
   (E) charming

2. The _____ restaurant customer was _____ rude to Ferdinand, but Ferdinand would only smile in return, choosing each time to hock a loogie in the man's food order.
   (A) irate, seldom
   (B) petulant, always
   (C) uncouth, once
   (D) obsequious, constantly
   (E) courteous, continually

CONTINUE ON NEXT PAGE ➡

3. David's heart _____ when he entered the house and was _____ by *Dateline NBC* investigative reporter Chris Hansen.
   - (A) soared, lauded
   - (B) skipped, berated
   - (C) quickened, assaulted
   - (D) burst, lacerated
   - (E) sank, confronted

4. Ironically, Kyle, who couldn't _____ his way out of a paper bag in real life, was already a level 20 Barbarian in the Dungeons & Dragons Tournament of Champions.
   - (A) lie
   - (B) pilfer
   - (C) improvise
   - (D) pillage
   - (E) embezzle

5. Gordon Ramsay informed the sous-chef that his frittatas were _____, his gazpacho tasted like deer piss, and his basil-poached wild bass had all the texture of _____!
   - (A) putrid, a light airy breeze
   - (B) permeable, dense charcoal
   - (C) delectable, a gentle moisturizer
   - (D) enchanting, a squirmy eel
   - (E) rancid, a soiled diaper

6. While there is certainly much _____ regarding the exact nature of Bruce Wayne and Dick Grayson's relationship, no one has ever proven anything one way or the other.
   - (A) conjecture
   - (B) amity
   - (C) nuance
   - (D) demagoguery
   - (E) gesticulation

7. When Amber _____ that Derek, the handsome quarterback, just snuck her a furtive glance as he passed her in the hall, she thought she would, like, oh my God, just totally die!
   - (A) exclaimed
   - (B) eked
   - (C) obviated
   - (D) pined
   - (E) discerned

8. Their _____ game of "Are we there yet?" was more than Mr. Williams could _____; he snapped and drove the car into an embankment.
   - (A) inane, bear
   - (B) perspicacious, endure
   - (C obtuse, comprehend
   - (D) churlish, stomach
   - (E) trademark, suffer

CONTINUE ON NEXT PAGE ➡

Questions 9–12 are based on the following passages.

Passage 1

Beauty and the Geek is a reality TV show that pairs a group of geeks with a group of beauties and pits them in challenges that
Line serve to expand their horizons and promote
5 their personal growth. Both beauties and geeks interact with each other in ways they had previously not thought possible, and each person gains insight into the others in the group, and themselves. Every con-
10 testant benefits from the experience and comes out a winner, regardless of which team actually receives the monetary prize at the end. *Beauty and the Geek* is a breath-taking social experiment, and is a rare ex-
15 ample of the power of television being used for public good.

Passage 2

Geeks exist for one purpose and one purpose alone, and that is to fix my computer and then go back to the cubicle from which
20 they came. What are these TV producers thinking? They're messing with the basic underlying fabric of our society. If beauties start to believe they have any self-worth outside of their rockin' bods, imagine the

25 effect on business, from the fashion industry, to the cosmetics industry, to the diet industry, to eating disorder clinics. Advertising would be a total disaster—how can you expect to sell anything without gratuitous T&A? And
30 can you imagine if all geeks were taught they could actually interact with beauties without having to hand them any singles? The entire economy would simply collapse. This show is just playing with fire.

9. The author of Passage 1 suggests that every contestant is a winner because they each
    (A) at least win a consolation prize
    (B) appear on TV and become reality stars
    (C) try new things and grow as individuals
    (D) are paired with members of the opposite sex
    (E) take part in a social experiment for the public good

CONTINUE ON NEXT PAGE ➡

10. In the context of Passage 2, the general argument is made that large parts of the economy depend on which of the following?

    (A) Geeks in cubicles
    (B) Keeping interest rates low
    (C) T&A
    (D) Traditional gender stereotypes
    (E) Advertising in order to sell products

11. Which of the following best describes the relationship between the two passages?

    (A) Passage 2 expands on an issue that is explored in Passage 1.
    (B) Passage 1 provides a logical argument concerning a topic, while Passage 2 provides an emotional argument instead.
    (C) Passage 2 provides an extreme example of a subject discussed in Passage 1.
    (D) Passage 1 presents evidence that rebuts the argument made in Passage 2.
    (E) Passage 1 and Passage 2 offer two opposing viewpoints on the same subject.

12. The two passages differ in opinion in that the author of Passage 1

    (A) seems to care more about people, while the author of Passage 2 seems to care more about money
    (B) believes *Beauty and the Geek* is a good show, while the author of Passage 2 doesn't watch it
    (C) desires social experimentation, while the author of Passage 2 prefers the status quo
    (D) wants to talk to beautiful women, while the author of Passage 2 wants to watch them in bathing suits running in slow motion down the beach
    (E) believes all people should live in harmony, while the author of Passage 2 believes in survival of the fittest

CONTINUE ON NEXT PAGE

Questions 13–24 are based on the following passage.

According to *Forbes* magazine, there were 946 billionaires in the world in 2007, 153 more than in the previous year. Think
Line about that—there were 153 more billionaires
5 in the last year alone. Not millionaires— billionaires, with a capital *B*. It was reported that a good number of these new billionaires earned their profits from soaring oil prices. Think about that the next time you fill your
10 gas tank. Or not—it's probably best not to think about it. I guess it literally pays to be friends with Dick Cheney.

Man, oh man. A billion dollars—what does that number even mean? It's like my four-
15 year-old son who says a jillion, or kajillion—it means nothing. It's just some mind-boggling large number. He says, "I love you a jillion times," and I say, "I love you a jillion and one." I know, it's sweet. Then he says, "I love
20 you a kajillion times," and I say, "I love you a kajillion and one." Still sweet, but just starting to get a little bit competitive, you know, like we need to one up each other. Next he says, "I love you a jillion kajillion times," thinking
25 he's got me, but then I say, "I love you a jillion kajillion and one." On and on it goes until he starts crying. Poor little guy doesn't know about infinity yet.

So when exactly is enough, enough?
30 Shouldn't there be a point where you say, "I don't need any more money? How could I possibly need any more money? I don't even know what to do with all the money I have now." No, people aren't like that. More
35 likely you say, "Okay, I'm just going to make one billion and then I'll stop." Then when you reach the billion it's, "Okay, two billion. Two

billion and that's all." Then it's, "Ah, but you know with inflation and taxes . . . OK, five
40 billion. Five billion is what I need." Until finally, it's, "Ah, screw it. Keep it coming. Daddy needs 50 million new pairs of shoes!"

What does one do with a billion dollars, anyway? I suppose if you're Michael Jackson
45 you can start inviting underage boys to sleep in your bed again, but I don't have any expensive habits. I wouldn't even know what to do. Build a golden toilet? What? I really wouldn't even know what to do. Of course,
50 my ex-wife would. She'd know what to do— you can bet on that. She and her team of lawyers would be all over that money like flies on a carcass—which is what I'd be after they were through with me.

55 I think it's funny how, even at the very top, there's still a ranking. It's not enough to have a billion dollars; we have to know who is number one. Topping the billionaires list for the 13th year in a row is Microsoft's Bill
60 Gates, with an estimated net worth listed at 56 billion dollars. That must really piss off all the other billionaires—a nerdy little pipsqueak making more than any of them. Can you imagine all the billionaire business
65 tycoons completely infuriated sitting around on their piles of money? Which is of course what business tycoons do—sit around on piles of money. When you've got so much of it, you might as well use it for furniture, right?
70 A bed of hundreds, a matching twenties table and chairs, a onesy sofa—imagine the irony of scrounging around in a onesy sofa, and exclaiming, "Oh look, a quarter!" Ah, the life of a billionaire.

75 I wonder if there's some Billionaire's Club, an actual physical club that you can join only if you have a billion dollars. It's probably like

CONTINUE ON NEXT PAGE ➡

a fraternity where the new guy first has to go through a hazing. Right now, they're putting
80 number 946 through the spanking machine. Then they're going to make him run naked through the grounds, and when he falls asleep they're going to shave his privates. Finally, he'll make it through and they'll teach
85 him the secret handshake, but everybody will still act all snobby and look down on him at first, always picking him last at the exclusive golf tournaments. Right now, one of the top billionaires is saying, "All right, I
90 guess I'll take 946. Hey, nice five-iron. Sure you can afford it?"

13. In the context of this passage, the author can primarily be described as
(A) incensed by the wealth disparity between the billionaires of the world and the rest of society
(B) wistful concerning the state of affairs in his own personal life
(C) fascinated by the concept of what it means to own a billion dollars and what it must be like to be a billionaire
(D) fully engrossed with the *Forbes* annual ranking of billionaires, relating personally to it
(E) captivated by the fact that the number of billionaires is growing, and wishing that he could join their ranks

14. In line 7, "good" most nearly means
(A) positive
(B) first-class
(C) sizeable
(D) well-behaved
(E) inordinate

15. The author writes "best not to think about it" (lines 10–11) most likely because
(A) most people get angry when they realize that a few individuals are gaining so much wealth off of something causing suffering to so many people
(B) the price of crude oil is just too complicated to comprehend
(C) soon enough the price of gasoline will come back down again
(D) while one might have to pay more in gas prices, one can also make a lot of money by investing in energy stocks
(E) one should keep one's eyes on the road at all times while driving

16. From the passage's second paragraph, one may deduce that
(A) a jillion is less than a billion
(B) a jillion is less than a gazillion
(C) a jillion is greater than a gazillion
(D) a jillion is less than a kajillion
(E) a jillion is greater than a kajillion

CONTINUE ON NEXT PAGE ➡

17. Lines 35–42 ("Okay, I'm just going to
. . . shoes!") describe
    (A) an example concerning the effective
        influence of mind over matter
    (B) an asserted theory of continuous
        financial market expansion
    (C) an illustration of the suspected
        psychological progression of
        individuals over time
    (D) a case study of an increasing
        cultural phenomenon
    (E) a demonstration of a contended
        physical principle involving affluent
        persons

18. The common point of both the second
    and fourth paragraph is that
    (A) the author's home life is nowhere
        near picture perfect
    (B) a billion dollars can be used to
        purchase almost countless
        material goods and services
    (C) a billion dollars can be used to
        support extremely unhealthy
        habits
    (D) it is very difficult for a person to
        count up to a billion
    (E) the notion of a billion dollars is
        basically unfathomable to the
        average person

19. The author of this passage went
    through a divorce that he would most
    likely characterize as
    (A) amicable
    (B) acrimonious
    (C) pithy
    (D) triumphant
    (E) insipid

20. In line 55, "funny" most nearly means
    (A) courageous
    (B) poignant
    (C) witty
    (D) fascinating
    (E) elating

21. In lines 72–73, the "irony" refers to
    (A) someone very rich owning furniture
        that is actually made out of money
    (B) being uncomfortable while sitting in
        furniture that is clearly extremely
        expensive
    (C) someone listening to an Alanis
        Morissette song
    (D) someone very rich having to search
        for loose change in a sofa
    (E) searching for loose change in
        furniture that is itself made out of
        money

22. If the author of this passage were to
    become a billionaire, his first purchase
    would be
    (A) a new pair of shoes
    (B) an expensive habit
    (C) a golden toilet
    (D) a lawyer
    (E) uncertain to determine from the
        passage

CONTINUE ON NEXT PAGE ➡

23. The author of the passage would most likely agree with which of the following statements concerning billionaires?
    (A) At the end of the day, billionaires are still human, with human foibles.
    (B) Billionaires are much too greedy and are the cause of much strife in the world.
    (C) Most billionaires inherit their wealth, which puts them at a distinct advantage over the rest of society.
    (D) Most billionaires are men who join the same fraternity.
    (E) Billionaires recline on piles of money.

24. One underlying assumption made throughout most of the passage is that billionaires are
    (A) predominantly male
    (B) extremely parsimonious
    (C) by and large, tall and white
    (D) munificent in nature
    (E) quite often out of touch with reality

S T O P
IF YOU FINISH BEFORE THE TIME ALLOTTED, YOU MAY
CHECK YOUR WORK IN *THIS SECTION ONLY*.

Critical Reading Practice Section 3

19 QUESTIONS

TIME: 20 MINUTES

DIRECTIONS: In the following sentences, each _____ indicates a word is missing. From among the five answer choices, choose the word, or set of words, that <u>best</u> fits the meaning of the sentence as a whole.

Oh my God—are you kidding me? Fill in the ____ing blanks!

1. When Carla _____ Gavin _____ her chest, she told him to take a picture so the image would last longer.
   (A) missed, staring at
   (B) noticed, shunning
   (C) ignored, observing
   (D) discovered, disregarding
   (E) caught, ogling

2. Worried he would lose street cred with his fans, the Gangsta rapper _____ the fact that he was raised in Beverly Hills—not on the mean streets of Compton.
   (A) concealed
   (B) expedited
   (C) proved
   (D) disproved
   (E) appraised

CONTINUE ON NEXT PAGE ➡

3. Tony was _____ at first upon receiving Chuck the Repo Man's call, but soon became _____ when he realized the call was simply meant as a distraction.
   (A) flattered, engaged
   (B) puzzled, irate
   (C) bothered, annoyed
   (D) furious, enlightened
   (E) distracted, indifferent

4. Lexi found herself in quite a _____; she had already agreed to go to the dance with Dean, but that was before Jake asked, and Jake was much hotter.
   (A) hegemony
   (B) gainsay
   (C) quandary
   (D) moribund
   (E) sophistry

5. _____ Triple-Crown winner Seattle Slew died at the ripe old age of 28, but the famous black stallion will live on in the hundreds of prize-winning horses he _____, and beginning next week, in Seattle Slew Glue.
   (A) Prosaic, routed
   (B) Noteworthy, inspired
   (C) Malevolent, yielded
   (D) Legendary, sired
   (E) Resonant, smote

6. Rose had absolutely no intention of eating right and going to the gym; she _____ that liposuction _____ the need for diet and exercise.
   (A) believed, obviated
   (B) denied, assuaged
   (C) surmised, necessitated
   (D) edified, prevaricated
   (E) doubted, forestalled

CONTINUE ON NEXT PAGE ➡

DIRECTIONS: The two passages below are followed by questions related to their content and the relationship between the two passages. Answer the questions based on what is <u>written</u> in the passage, and on what may be <u>implied</u> from the passage.

Burger, Flip, Repeat.

Questions 7–19 are based on the following passages.

Passage 1

Her beauty shines forth like the sun, illuminating the darkness that surrounds her, allowing each in her wake to bask in her infinite
Line glory. In her possession lies the power of a
5 thousand Helen of Troys—a million ships for her honor. She is a vision; she is a goddess. Surely, she is Venus personified.

What man can resist her magnificent splendor? Her eyes, like two precious sap-
10 phires, sparkle dazzlingly in the moonlight. Her ruby lips purse, ever so slightly, and yet melt a winter's day. Her smile, a glimmering beacon of pearls, flashes forth as she spins, like a lighthouse to the lonely ships of
15 the night. Her creamy hide glistens softly in the morning dew. She glides with grace unmatched, her mountains heaving with every step in her flower of youth.

He sees her and is transfixed. Immedi-
20 ately, all that had been uncertain becomes clear and secure. Time and space collide as one, and all at once, he knows the meaning of his life. To adore is his purpose; to worship is his mission. It is a calling of joy and
25 he revels in his blessing.

And yet, he wonders, can there be more? A simple look, a fleeting touch, or perhaps, he dares to dream, an exploration of the pas-

sions of forever. No, he must not think them,
30 let alone speak such lofty dreams as these. And yet he wonders, and yet he wonders.

With all the courage in his spirit, he asks. Again and again, he asks. It must be yes—it can only be yes—for he cannot endure the
35 alternative. His question shoots forth, traveling a journey unknown, to reach her he knows not how, and yet he knows that it will. Now he waits with bated breath, with a love in his heart that knows no earthly bounds,
40 aching with all of his eternal soul for that single yes to complete his very being. He awaits her reply.

Passage 2

For the last time, I am not going to the prom with you, you freak! Leave me alone!
45 You asked me out once, that's fine. One hundred times in two days is not. That's called stalking. Now, I have tried being nice to you, but you clearly can't take a hint, so here's the deal. First of all, I don't like you,
50 and I don't find you attractive in the least. You're a Troll doll with zits. Second of all, you're, like, in the marching band and you play a tuba. A tuba! Wake up and smell the reality, you dweeb. Just because your video
55 game avatar can get a date doesn't mean you can too. I mean, really, get serious. Finally, and I didn't want to have to say this, but your feet stink. I don't know if it's some

CONTINUE ON NEXT PAGE ➡

kind of grody fungus you have, or what, but
60 they reek. Trust me—I'm not even exagger-
ating. People can smell you a mile away. You
really need to see a doctor or something.

And, OMG, don't even get me started on
the e-mail. Can you say *Cheeseball*? Creamy
65 hide? What am I? A dead cow? Heaving
mountains? Flower of youth? That is just
gross, you perv. Passions of forever—I want
to barf forever. Listen, and listen closely, because I am going to give you some free ad-
70 vice right now. If you ever want to lose your
virginity, stop saying stuff like that!

You want my reply? I'll give you my reply.
Get lost, creep. I can't be any clearer than
this. I don't want to be your girlfriend. I don't
75 want to be your prom date. I don't want to
go out with you. I don't want to make out
with you. I don't want to kiss you. I don't
want to be your friend. I don't want to be
your buddy. I don't want to hang out with
80 you. I don't even want to talk to you. I don't
want to have anything to do with you what-
soever. LEAVE ME ALONE!

E-mail me again and I'm telling Principal
Radford.

7. In context of the two passages,
   Passage 1 can most accurately be
   described as
   (A) a love letter to a romantic partner
   (B) a flowery passage from a romance
       novel
   (C) an unwelcome request for a prom
       date
   (D) an e-mail
   (E) a passage from a science fiction
       novel

8. In line 11, "purse" most nearly means
   (A) tighten up like a vise
   (B) an expensive handbag, such as a
       Gucci
   (C) press together
   (D) prize winnings
   (E) blow

9. The woman described in Passage 1 is
   compared to which of the following?
       I. A mythological figure
       II. Morning dew
       III. Moonlight
   (A) I only
   (B) II only
   (C) I and II only
   (D) II and III only
   (E) I, II, and III

10. In Passage 1, references are made to
    all of the following body parts of "She"
    EXCEPT her
    (A) eyes
    (B) teeth
    (C) breasts
    (D) arms
    (E) skin

11. In Passage 1, "He" is unsatisfied with
    (A) waiting for an answer to his question,
        and asks someone else instead
    (B) worshipping "She" only from afar,
        and desires a closer physical
        relationship
    (C) having only the mind of "She," and
        desires her body as well
    (D) sharing "She" with others, and
        desires her only for himself
    (E) a simple look, and desires a fleeting
        touch as well

CONTINUE ON NEXT PAGE

12. Throughout Passage 1, "She" most likely refers to
   (A) a beautiful mountain range
   (B) Helen of Troy
   (C) love in human form
   (D) the goddess of love
   (E) the author of Passage 2

13. In line 55, "avatar" most nearly means
   (A) persona
   (B) guru
   (C) high-score
   (D) antagonist
   (E) cohort

14. In the context of Passage 2, the author employs the term "Cheeseball" (line 64) to voice the opinion that her suitor is a
   (A) rotund sloth
   (B) connoisseur of fine cheeses
   (C) stalker
   (D) sappy writer
   (E) Troll doll with zits

15. Which of the following most accurately describes a stated reason why the suitor in Passage 2 was rejected?
   (A) He plays a musical instrument.
   (B) He has a possible medical condition.
   (C) He is destitute.
   (D) His physical exterior is lacking.
   (E) He didn't say "please."

16. In the context of Passage 2, the suitor is advised to do which of the following in order to increase his chances at a sexual experience?
   (A) Bathe more often, use an acne cleanser, stop playing the tuba, and stop playing video games
   (B) Date more often, be confident, be attentive to her needs, and stop trying so hard
   (C) Ask women out using colloquial speech, stop being corny, stop referring to their body parts, and stop being salacious
   (D) Drop out of the marching band, stop playing the tuba, pick up a guitar, and start a rock and roll band
   (E) Stop stalking, stop trying so hard, stop being sexually suggestive, and just be himself

17. The author of Passage 2 would be most shocked to see her suitor at the prom on a date with
   (A) his older sister
   (B) a gorgeous paid escort
   (C) the least attractive girl in school
   (D) the prom queen
   (E) a fellow tuba player

CONTINUE ON NEXT PAGE ➡

18. Should the author of Passage 2 spot the author of Passage 1 in a hallway, the author of Passage 2 would most likely
(A) congratulate the author of Passage 1 on getting published
(B) turn around and walk away in order to avoid the author of Passage 1
(C) ask the author of Passage 1 to a formal debate
(D) kill the author of Passage 1
(E) beg the author of Passage 1 to leave her alone

19. The author of Passage 1 and the author of Passage 2 agree that, in terms of the "He" and "She" employed in Passage 1,
(A) "He" has been relentlessly stalking "She"
(B) "She" is worthy of being compared to precious gemstones
(C) the question "He" asked will remain unanswered
(D) "She" is actually an imaginary person
(E) normally, "He" should not even be talking to "She"

S T O P
IF YOU FINISH BEFORE THE TIME ALLOTTED, YOU MAY
CHECK YOUR WORK IN *THIS SECTION ONLY*.

Writing Practice Section 1

35 QUESTIONS

TIME: 25 MINUTES

DIRECTIONS: In the following sentences, a portion of the sentence, or the entire sentence, is underlined. The answer choices provide different ways of phrasing the underlined portion of the sentence. From among the five answer choices, choose the phrasing that results in the best overall sentence, paying attention to grammar, word choices, punctuation, and sentence construction. Your selection should provide the most effective sentence—one that is clear, precise, and not awkward or ambiguous. Choice (A) is simply a repeat of the original phrasing, so if you believe the original phrasing provides a better result than any of the alternatives, you should choose (A) as your answer.

In other words, these sentences might be broken, but you can fix them by replacing the underlined parts with one of the five choices. Pick the choice that makes the best overall sentence.

Just so you know, the smart kids already read these directions before taking the test. Why didn't you? You've wasted, like, a full minute already. And yet you're still reading. Fix the sentences already!

CONTINUE ON NEXT PAGE

1. The Internet <u>turned 38 years old during the course of</u> this year, and it is still a virgin, living at home with its parents.
   (A) turned 38 years old during the course of
   (B) has turned 38 years old during the course of
   (C) turned 38 year old
   (D) turned 38 year old during the course of
   (E) turned 38 years old

2. Of all the Flavor Flav girls, she was <u>definitely the more skanky</u>.
   (A) definitely the more skanky
   (B) definitely the most skankiest
   (C) the more skanky definitely
   (D) definitely the most skanky
   (E) definitely more skanky

3. My parents, Brad and Angelina, <u>went to Vietnam and all they got me was this lousy brother</u>.
   (A) went to Vietnam and all they got me was this lousy brother
   (B) went to Vietnam, all they got me was this lousy brother
   (C) went to Vietnam, this lousy brother was all they got me
   (D) went to Vietnam; and all they got me was this lousy brother
   (E) went to Vietnam; and this lousy brother was all they got me

4. At the United Nations Global Summit on Young People, 180 nations pledged to make the world a better place for kids, <u>and then were going back to killing each other</u>.
   (A) and then were going back to killing each other
   (B) and then gone back to killing each other
   (C) and then going back to killing each other
   (D) and then went back to killing each other
   (E) then gone back to killing each other

5. <u>They say that no one can hear it when you fart in space.</u>
   (A) They say that no one can hear it when you fart in space.
   (B) When in space, they say that no one can hear it when you fart.
   (C) In space, no one can hear you fart.
   (D) They say that they can not hear you fart in space.
   (E) They say that if you fart in space, no one can hear the sound of it.

CONTINUE ON NEXT PAGE ➡

6. <u>Maya purchased them because she thought they were pretty</u>, but she had no idea that the skirt made her butt look like two Great Danes fighting over a milk bone.
   - (A) Maya purchased them because she thought they were pretty
   - (B) It was purchased by Maya because she thought it was pretty
   - (C) Maya purchased it because she thought they were pretty
   - (D) They were purchased by Maya because she thought they were pretty
   - (E) Maya purchased it because she thought it was pretty

7. I like to celebrate Halloween each year by <u>shutting off all the lights and remain very quiet</u>.
   - (A) shutting off all the lights and remain very quiet
   - (B) shut off all the lights and remain very quiet
   - (C) shut off all the lights and remaining very quiet
   - (D) shutting off all the lights and remaining very quiet
   - (E) shutting off all the lights and to remain very quiet

8. Jesus may love you, <u>but all I just want to be friends</u>.
   - (A) but all I just want to be friends
   - (B) but I just want to be friends
   - (C) but all I want just to be friends
   - (D) and I just want to be friends
   - (E) and all I just want is to be friends

9. <u>I truly apologize for squeezing your ass during the huddle, I totally thought you were Antoine.</u>
   - (A) I truly apologize for squeezing your ass during the huddle, I totally thought you were Antoine.
   - (B) I truly apologize for squeezing your ass during the huddle; as I totally thought you were Antoine.
   - (C) I truly apologize for squeezing your ass during the huddle; I totally thought you were Antoine.
   - (D) I truly apologize for squeezing your ass during the huddle, and I totally thought you were Antoine.
   - (E) Because I totally thought you were Antoine, I truly apologize for squeezing your ass during the huddle.

10. The popular Internet teen social networking site has over 80 million members, <u>included among them are</u> thousands upon thousands of registered sex offenders.
    - (A) included among them are
    - (B) for which there are included
    - (C) including
    - (D) and they also included
    - (E) to which we include

CONTINUE ON NEXT PAGE ➡

11. Although he claimed his rendition of "I Love You, You Love Me" was completely innocent, the undercover police officer arrested Barney the Dinosaur last night for propositioning her.

(A) the undercover police officer arrested Barney the Dinosaur last night for propositioning her

(B) the undercover police officer, who was propositioned last night, arrested Barney the Dinosaur

(C) Barney the Dinosaur, who propositioned the undercover police officer last night, was arrested

(D) Barney the Dinosaur, for propositioning the undercover police officer, was arrested last night

(E) Barney the Dinosaur was arrested last night for propositioning the undercover police officer

CONTINUE ON NEXT PAGE ➡

DIRECTIONS: Each of the following sentences either contain one (and only one) error or no error at all. The error, if there is one, is located in one of the underlined portions of the sentence, and each underlined portion is labeled with a letter. If the sentence contains an error, choose the letter corresponding to the underlined portion that would need to be changed in order to fix the sentence. If the sentence is correct, choose (E) as your answer.

In other words, find the error in the sentence or choose (E) if the sentence is correct.

Still reading these directions, huh? Sure, why not? You have all the time in the world. It's not like there's a time limit for these sections, right? What's that? There is? Then why are you still here? Errors—go find them. Shoo!

12. <u>Although</u> <u>he</u> never lost a single game
    A   B
of Twister, Mr. Fantastic <u>is</u> quite often
                     C
accused of <u>cheating</u>. <u>No error</u>
         D   E

13. I believe that once an athlete <u>thanks</u>
                           A
Jesus for a win, <u>one</u> should be
          B
immediately disqualified for <u>using</u> a
                       C
performance <u>enhancer</u>. <u>No error</u>
        D   E

14. Teenage Casper desperately wished
that <u>him</u> and Wendy <u>could be</u> more <u>than</u>
    A   B   C
just <u>friends</u>. <u>No error</u>
    D   E

15. Mary-Kate and Ashley <u>went on</u> the
                     A
exact same diet, but somehow Mary-
Kate <u>lost</u> much more weight <u>than</u>
    B   C
<u>Ashley's diet</u>. <u>No error</u>
   D   E

CONTINUE ON NEXT PAGE ➡

150

16. The paranormal detective <u>was</u> in
                            A

   particularly high spirits until he

   <u>discovered</u> that <u>his</u> Sasquatch sighting
      B   C

   <u>were in fact</u> just a case of Robin Williams
      D

   out on a camping trip. <u>No error</u>
                              E

17. <u>On</u> a national day of prayer, people get
      A

   all dressed up, <u>take</u> their families to
                      B

   church, and <u>they would also</u> <u>pray</u> that
                   C   D

   their kids don't get hit on by a priest.

   <u>No error</u>
      E

18. <u>Hannah's parents and Julie's parents</u>
                      A

   both split up around the same time,

   <u>but</u> Hannah, due to <u>a</u> bitter custody
      B   C

   battle, received way more presents than

   <u>Julie's divorce.</u> <u>No error</u>
         D   E

19. Yugi realized something <u>was amiss</u>
                              A

   with his <u>playing</u> deck when, <u>instead of</u>
              B   C

   drawing the Dark Magician, he <u>pulls out</u>
                                    D

   a seven of diamonds. <u>No error</u>
                            E

20. The <u>most</u> common <u>side effect</u> <u>include</u>
         A   B   C

   nausea, diarrhea, <u>and sudden death</u>.
                        D

   <u>No error</u>
      E

21. <u>One</u> cannot help <u>to</u> wonder if Bill Gates
      A   B

   tells his old classmates to "suck it"

   <u>every time</u> he <u>peruses</u> his high school
      C   D

   yearbook. <u>No error</u>
                 E

22. The limited-edition <u>commemorative</u>
                            A

   Jamaican coins, featuring

   <u>the likeness of</u> late reggae star
         B

   Bob Marley, <u>comes in</u> three different
                  C

   varieties—gold, silver, <u>and ganja</u>.
                              D

   <u>No error</u>
      E

CONTINUE ON NEXT PAGE

23. When the <u>loyal worker</u> created a
                   A
    product <u>that</u> could be made just one
              B
    time and then resold over and over

    again <u>without any more effort</u>,
                      C
    <u>he was rewarded</u> by the company with
           D
    a pink slip. <u>No error</u>
                       E

24. <u>Apologizing profusely</u> to Harry for
        A
    <u>entering his</u> room without knocking,
        B
    Dumbledore graciously <u>took his leave</u>,
                                 C
    shut the door <u>behind him</u>, bit his fist,
                      D
    and remarked, "Gryffindor: 100 points."

    <u>No error</u>
        E

25. Britney <u>solemn</u> <u>vowed</u> that <u>from now on</u>
                A   B   C
    she will do her laundry before she

    <u>goes out</u> clubbing. <u>No error</u>
        D   E

26. Scientists <u>have discovered</u> that
                     A
    pollutants from as far away as Asia

    <u>have been crossing</u> oceans, reaching
              B
    all the way to the East Coast, <u>and</u>, in a
                                       C
    related story, if you hurry to your local

    video store, <u>one</u> can still catch *Around*
                     D
    the World in Eighty Days, starring Jackie

    Chan. <u>No error</u>
              E

27. The <u>disconcerted</u> apparition asked the
            A
    ghost whisperer to <u>speak out</u>,
                           B
    <u>as he could not hear</u> a single word
              C
    she <u>was saying</u>. <u>No error</u>
            D   E

28. Heather insisted she was

    <u>acting altruistically</u>, and <u>it</u> wasn't
        A   B
    <u>her</u> fault that the person she liked
    C
    helping most was <u>herself</u>. <u>No error</u>
                         D   E

CONTINUE ON NEXT PAGE ➡

29. Paula did not <u>have the heart</u> to
$\qquad$ A

comment on William's pitch, <u>but</u>
$\qquad\qquad$ B

Simon called <u>him</u> grating and offensive,
$\qquad$ C

and proclaimed that the only way

William would ever make money

through singing is if people

<u>paid him to stop.</u> <u>No error</u>
$\qquad$ D $\qquad\qquad$ E

CONTINUE ON NEXT PAGE ➡

DIRECTIONS: The following passage is an early draft of an essay that needs revising. Read the passage and answer the questions that follow. Questions can be about improving a particular sentence or sentences, or they can be about improving the general organization and structure of the essay. For each question, choose the best answer among the answer choices, following the requirements of standard written English.

Read a passage; answer questions. By any chance, were you ever dropped on your head as a child? Just wondering.

Questions 30–35 are based on the following passage.

The following is a first draft of a thank-you note for a birthday gift.

(1) Mom is making me write you a thank-you note, so that is what I am doing. (2) Thank you, Grandma, for giving me a pair of underwear, you must have bought at the dollar store, instead of the Bratz doll I wanted. (3) My friends are laughing at me, and Tina called me Granny Panties. (4) The whole school knows.

(5) According to Mom, I should be nice to you. (6) You are old and losing your brain. (7) Anyway, she said I won't be seeing you much anymore because Dad is buying you a new house and you are moving away. (8) I hope you are moving to Alaska.

(9) She is very sad and she is crying a lot, but I don't know why. (10) I am very happy. (11) I am very happy because now I can get my own room. (12) I will have to buy some air freshener to get rid of the old lady smell.

30. In context, which is the best way to deal with sentence 2 (reproduced as follows)?
Thank you, Grandma, for giving me a pair of underwear, you must have bought at the dollar store, instead of the Bratz doll I wanted.
(A) Leave it as is.
(B) Insert "which" before "you must have bought".
(C) Delete "must have".
(D) Delete "I wanted".
(E) Change "wanted" to "want".

CONTINUE ON NEXT PAGE ➡

31. In context, which is the best way to revise and combine sentences 5 and 6 (reproduced as follows)?

    According to Mom, I should be nice to you. You are old and losing your brain.

    (A) According to Mom, I should be nice to you, and you are old and losing your brain.
    (B) According to Mom, I should be nice to you, but you are old and losing your brain.
    (C) According to Mom, I should be nice to you because you are old and losing your brain.
    (D) I should be nice to you, according to Mom, you are old and losing your brain.
    (E) You are old and losing your brain, therefore according to Mom, I should be nice to you.

32. In context, which of the following actions to sentence 9 (reproduced as follows) offers the most improvement?

    She is very sad and she is crying a lot, but I don't know why.

    (A) Leaving it as is.
    (B) Replacing "she" with "Mom".
    (C) Replacing "she" with "Grandma".
    (D) Deleting "she is".
    (E) Replacing "She" with "Mom".

33. What should be done with sentence 10 (reproduced as follows)?

    I am very happy.

    (A) Leave it as is.
    (B) Insert "In contrast," at the beginning.
    (C) Add "and smiling" at the end.
    (D) Move it after sentence 12.
    (E) Delete it.

34. In context, what should be done with sentence 12 (reproduced as follows)?

    I will have to buy some air freshener to get rid of the old lady smell.

    (A) Leave it as is.
    (B) Change "have" to "need".
    (C) Change "old lady smell" to "smell of old lady".
    (D) Insert "Although, first" at the beginning.
    (E) Delete "some".

35. Which of the following is best to add after sentence 12 in order to conclude the note?

    (A) Afterwards, I will throw a party.
    (B) Anyway, I think I have written enough so I will stop now.
    (C) After all is said and done, I forgive you.
    (D) That's all, folks.
    (E) If I may be honest, I will surely miss you, Grandma.

S T O P

IF YOU FINISH BEFORE THE TIME ALLOTTED, YOU MAY
CHECK YOUR WORK IN *THIS SECTION ONLY*.

Writing Practice Section 2

14 QUESTIONS

TIME: 10 MINUTES

Here we go again. In case you hadn't noticed, these exact instructions appeared in the last practice section. Why are you reading them again? Hello? Anybody home?

1. Ozzy first tried to pee the fire out, but finally realized <u>one needed to call the fire department</u>.
   - (A) one needed to call the fire department
   - (B) he needs to call the fire department
   - (C) one needs to call the fire department
   - (D) he needed to call the fire department
   - (E) one needed to call out the fire department

CONTINUE ON NEXT PAGE ➡

156

2. Tiffany and Khandi became anorexic <u>soon after they decided to become a model</u>.
   - (A) soon after they decided to become a model
   - (B) soon after they decide to become models
   - (C) as soon as modeling is what they decided to do
   - (D) because a model is what they decided to become
   - (E) soon after they decided to become models

3. <u>Finding the grocery store fresh out of turkey on Thanksgiving Day, the video store rented me the latest Rob Schneider movie instead.</u>
   - (A) Finding the grocery store fresh out of turkey on Thanksgiving Day, the video store rented me the latest Rob Schneider movie instead.
   - (B) Finding the grocery store fresh out of turkey on Thanksgiving Day, at the video store I rented the latest Rob Schneider movie instead.
   - (C) Finding the grocery store fresh out of turkey on Thanksgiving Day, I went to the video store and rented the latest Rob Schneider movie instead.
   - (D) While at the video store, I found the grocery store fresh out of turkey on Thanksgiving Day, so I rented the latest Rob Schneider movie instead.
   - (E) Finding the grocery store fresh out of turkey on Thanksgiving Day, the latest Rob Schneider movie was rented from the video store instead.

4. The word "Internet" is believed to have come from the Latin words "Inter" and "Net," <u>as they mean</u> "Star Trek" and "porn."
   - (A) as they mean
   - (B) the meanings of which are
   - (C) for which it is meant
   - (D) they mean
   - (E) which mean

5. Disneyland in Hong Kong is much like Disneyland here, except <u>each night</u> the Main Street Parade all the cartoon animals are eaten.
   - (A) each night
   - (B) each night after
   - (C) but once each night after
   - (D) once upon the completion of
   - (E) only the difference being that after

6. Doctors are urging younger, college-aged women to receive regular breast exams, and <u>insist that drinking oneself stupid and getting felt up</u> by a bunch of frat boys does not qualify.
   - (A) insist that drinking oneself stupid and getting felt up
   - (B) insist that to drink oneself stupid and got felt up
   - (C) insist that when you drink yourself stupid and get felt up
   - (D) drink yourself stupid and get felt up
   - (E) they insist that when you drink oneself stupid and you get felt up

CONTINUE ON NEXT PAGE

7. A top U.S. commander said that Osama bin Laden maybe hiding in eastern Afghanistan, or possibly western Afghanistan, or Pakistan, or maybe Yemen, or even somewhere else entirely.
   - (A) A top U.S. commander said that Osama bin Laden maybe hiding in eastern Afghanistan
   - (B) Osama bin Laden is maybe hiding in eastern Afghanistan, said a top U.S. commander
   - (C) A top U.S. commander said that Osama bin Laden maybe hidden in eastern Afghanistan
   - (D) A top U.S. commander said that Osama bin Laden may be hiding in eastern Afghanistan
   - (E) Osama bin Laden maybe hiding in eastern Afghanistan said a top U.S. commander

8. Researchers say that teenagers who are vegetarians are much healthier than other teens; that is, they're healthier until they become beaten up by the other teens for being different.
   - (A) they become beaten up by the other teens
   - (B) the other teens beat them up
   - (C) they are being beaten up by the other teens
   - (D) the other teens make them beaten up
   - (E) they will be beaten up by the other teens

9. Hilary Duff announced that a portion of all ticket sales from her upcoming concert tour will go toward charity, while going toward singing lessons will be the rest of the money.
   - (A) while going toward singing lessons will be the rest of the money
   - (B) while going toward the rest of the money will be singing lessons
   - (C) while the rest of the money will go toward singing lessons
   - (D) and going toward singing lessons will be the rest of the money
   - (E) and singing lessons will go toward the rest of the money

10. Scientists say that greenhouse gases are causing the Earth to heat up even faster than predicted, but luckily there is no cause for alarm because the fossil fuel industry refuses to except the existence of global warming.
   - (A) the fossil fuel industry refuses to except the existence of global warming
   - (B) the fossil fuel industry refuses to accept the existence of global warming
   - (C) refusing to except the existence of global warming is the fossil fuel industry
   - (D) the fossil fuel industry refused to except the existence of global warming
   - (E) the existence of global warming is being refused acceptance by the fossil fuel industry

CONTINUE ON NEXT PAGE

11. Gerald felt like <u>the bigger loser</u> of all when even MySpace Tom rejected his friendship.
    - (A) the bigger loser
    - (B) a bigger loser
    - (C) the biggest loser
    - (D) the bigger of the losers
    - (E) the big loser

12. Hulk Hogan was inducted into the World Wrestling Entertainment Hall of Fame, <u>his place is confirmed</u> as one of the all-time great fake sportsmen.
    - (A) his place is confirmed
    - (B) but this confirms his place
    - (C) to confirm his place
    - (D) thus confirming his place
    - (E) his place will be confirmed

13. <u>Courtney declared she would remain faithful to her virginity pledge; Dylan convinced her that prom night was an allowable exception.</u>
    - (A) Courtney declared she would remain faithful to her virginity pledge; Dylan convinced her that prom night was an allowable exception.
    - (B) Courtney declared she would remain faithful to her virginity pledge, but Dylan convinced her that prom night was an allowable exception.
    - (C) Courtney declared she would remain faithful to her virginity pledge; but Dylan convinced her that prom night was an allowable exception.
    - (D) Courtney declared she remained faithful to her virginity pledge, but Dylan convinced her that prom night was an allowable exception.
    - (E) Dylan convinced her that prom night was an allowable exception because Courtney declared she would remain faithful to her virginity pledge.

14. In the new FOX-TV reality series, *Who's Your Bastard?*, a pro-basketball player <u>must identify his</u> biological child from a group of ten extramarital offspring.
    - (A) must identify his
    - (B) must identify its
    - (C) must identify a
    - (D) identifies their
    - (E) must identify from his

S T O P

IF YOU FINISH BEFORE THE TIME ALLOTTED, YOU MAY
CHECK YOUR WORK IN *THIS SECTION ONLY*.

Mathematics Practice Section 1

20 QUESTIONS

TIME: 25 MINUTES

DIRECTIONS: For each question, choose the best answer from among the choices given. Please note:

1. All numbers are real numbers.
2. The domain of any function f is equal to the set of all real numbers x for which $f(x)$ is a real number, unless otherwise specified.
3. All figures are drawn as accurately as possible, unless specifically indicated that the figure is not drawn to scale.
4. All figures lie on a plane unless otherwise specified.
5. Calculators are permitted.

Answer math questions. Oooh, that was tough.

FYI, the smart kids already read these instructions before the test. How much time did you just waste here? Just saying . . .

1. If Rosie O'Donnell can eat a 20-pound turkey in 12 minutes, how many minutes would it take her, at that rate, to eat a 30-pound ham?
   - (A) 8
   - (B) 12
   - (C) 16
   - (D) 18
   - (E) 20

CONTINUE ON NEXT PAGE

2. Let x represent the number of *Cannabis* plants on Jerry's farm.
   If $420 = \frac{x - 420}{420}$, what is the value of x?

   (A) $\frac{420}{420}$

   (B) 420

   (C) 420 + 420

   (D) $(420)^2 + 420$

   (E) 420420

3. After paying rent and health expenses, Grandma has 5 dollars remaining from her Social Security check to buy food each week. Cans of Fancy Feast are on special, 6 for 2 dollars. How many cans of Fancy Feast can Grandma afford this week?
   (A) 4
   (B) 6
   (C) 10
   (D) 12
   (E) 15

4. The following two sets are defined as:
   I heart Brad = {Britney, Carla, Jen, Lance}
   I heart Denzel = {Kanisha, Lance, Shanaynay}
   Which of the following sets is equal to the intersection of I heart Brad and I heart Denzel?
   (A) {}
   (B) {Lance}
   (C) {Brad, Denzel}
   (D) {Carla, Lance}
   (E) {Britney, Carla, Jen, Lance, Kanisha, Shanaynay}

5.

In the preceding figure, if x, the length of the hypotenuse of the triangle, has a value of 5, what is the value of y?
(A) 2
(B) 4
(C) $x^2 - 9$
(D) 6
(E) $(34)^{1/2}$

CONTINUE ON NEXT PAGE ➡

6. After losing his job to outsourcing, Steven waits in line at the local unemployment office. There are 500 unemployed workers in front of Steven and the same number behind him. How many total unemployed are in the line?

(A) 999
(B) 1,000
(C) 1,001
(D) 1,002
(E) 1,003

7. Let x represent the amount of money Frankie borrows from Don Vito, and let y represent the amount of money Frankie pays Don Vito back. Come next Friday, if $x > y$, then the new amount Frankie would owe Don Vito would be $5x - 5y$. If $x - y = 5,000$ and next Friday has just arrived, how much does Frankie now owe Don Vito?

(A) 5,000
(B) 10,000
(C) 25,000
(D) 50,000
(E) The answer cannot be determined.

8. Tristan is at his girlfriend's house when she informs him that he's going to be a daddy. Tristan runs due north at an average rate of 8 miles per hour for a period of one hour and then runs due west at an average rate of 6 miles per hour for another hour. At the end of two hours, what is the straight-line distance (in miles) between Tristan and his starting point?

(A) 8
(B) 9.5
(C) 10
(D) 10.5
(E) 14

9.

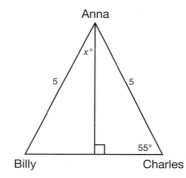

In the isosceles love triangle, what is the value of x?

(A) 15
(B) 17.5
(C) 20
(D) 35
(E) 55

CONTINUE ON NEXT PAGE ➡

10. Sixteen-year-old Kevin weighs 120 pounds at the beginning of the year. At the end of the year, after eating three meals a day at McDonalds, Kevin weighs 210 pounds and has developed Type II diabetes. Kevin's weight at the end of the year is what percent greater than his weight at the beginning of the year?

(A) $\frac{3}{4}$%

(B) $42\frac{6}{7}$%

(C) 75%

(D) 90%

(E) 210%

11. Not including Wong-Li, the average (arithmetic mean) score on a math test is 10 out of 100. Including Wong-Li, the average score is 12. There are 50 total students in the class. What score did Wong-Li receive on the math test?
(A) 12
(B) 60
(C) 99
(D) 100
(E) 110

12. A stripper's earnings are directly proportional to the size of her breast implants. If Suzie Woo earns $\frac{y}{2}$ dollars a year with her C-cups, how much can she earn in a year by going three times as big and changing her last name to Moo?

(A) $\frac{y}{6}$

(B) $\frac{y}{3}$

(C) y

(D) $\frac{3y}{2}$

(E) $3y$

13. There are 5 African-Americans in a police lineup, from which a Caucasian identifies a robbery suspect. Assuming all African-American people look alike to the Caucasian, what is the probability for a given person in the lineup to be identified?
(A) 0.2
(B) 0.25
(C) 0.5
(D) 1
(E) 20

CONTINUE ON NEXT PAGE ➡

14.

In the preceeding figure, what is the area of the censor bar?

(A) $x^{3/4}$
(B) x^2
(C) $2x^2 + 2x^{3/4}$
(D) $x^{3/2}$
(E) $x^{11/4}$

15. Alec Baldwin catches a flight to Los Angeles in order to chew out his teenage daughter. He leaves New York at noon eastern standard time (EST) and arrives in Los Angeles at 2:00 P.M. Pacific standard time (PST) on the same day. If it is noon PST when it is 3:00 P.M. EST, how many hours did Alec have to wait for his flight to reach Los Angeles before he could start berating his daughter in person?

(A) 2
(B) 3
(C) 5
(D) 6
(E) 8

16. Fourteen years ago, Ashton Kutcher was exactly half the age of his wife Demi Moore. The sum of their ages today is 76. How old will Ashton be in 20 years when he leaves Demi for her first-born daughter?

(A) 30
(B) 48
(C) 50
(D) 52
(E) 53

CONTINUE ON NEXT PAGE ➡

17. Let Donald Trump's current ego be represented by a cube with each edge length equal to s. If Trump's ego grows to a cube with each edge length equal to 3s, what is the ratio of the volume of Donald Trump's new ego to the volume of his current ego?
    (A) 3 to 1
    (B) 6s to 2
    (C) 9 to 1
    (D) 9π to 1
    (E) 27s to s

18. Prissy is 64 inches tall. She only dates guys who are more than 8 inches, and less than 12 inches, taller than her. Which of the following inequalities can be used to determine if a guy of height h inches would stand a shot with Prissy?
    (A) $|h - 52| < 24$
    (B) $|h - 64| < 12$
    (C) $|h - 72| < 4$
    (D) $|h - 74| < 2$
    (E) $|h - 76| < 12$

19. Halitosis Haley walks along a straight-line path in the xy-plane given by the equation, $y = 3x + 2$. Desperately trying to avoid her, Kyle walks away in a perpendicular straight line with slope m and y-intercept b. If the two lines intersect when $x = 3$, what is the value of b?

    (A) $-\frac{1}{3}$

    (B) $\frac{1}{3}$

    (C) 2

    (D) 11

    (E) 12

20. Suppose the amount of profit one can make from selling x T-shirts with the slogan "I'm not tired, I'm narcoleptic" is given by $\$\$x\$\$$, where $\$\$x\$\$$ is defined as $\$\$x\$\$ = x^2 - 2x$ for all $x \geq 0$. If $\$\$a - 2\$\$ = \$\$a\$\$$, what is the value of a?
    (A) 0
    (B) 1
    (C) 2
    (D) 3
    (E) 4

S T O P
IF YOU FINISH BEFORE THE TIME ALLOTTED, YOU MAY
CHECK YOUR WORK IN *THIS SECTION ONLY.*

Mathematics Practice Section 2

18 QUESTIONS

TIME: 25 MINUTES

DIRECTIONS: For each question, choose the best answer from among the choices given. Please note:

1. All numbers are real numbers.
2. The domain of any function f is equal to the set of all real numbers x for which $f(x)$ is a real number, unless otherwise specified.
3. All figures are drawn as accurately as possible, unless specifically indicated that the figure is not drawn to scale.
4. All figures lie on a plane unless otherwise specified.
5. Calculators are permitted.

Blah, blah, blah. Now you've wasted another minute. Bye-bye, Ivy League! Just answer the freaking math questions already!

CONTINUE ON NEXT PAGE

1. Plane ticket for African research trip:
$1,800

Twenty packs of Trojans for study on teaching safe sex to primates:
$120

Beaker of pheromones to replace the one you clumsily dropped all over yourself:
$4

Not catching AIDS from a monkey:
priceless

What is the ratio of the cost of the beaker to the cost of one pack of Trojans?
(A) 1:30
(B) 2:3
(C) 1:1
(D) 3:2
(E) 30:1

2. GAS PASSAGE IN THE HARRIS HOUSEHOLD

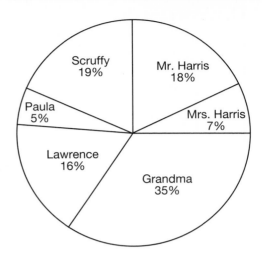

The pie chart shows the breakdown of random gas passage in the Harris household. If gas was just randomly passed, what is the probability that it originated from someone other than Scruffy?
(A) 0.0081
(B) 0.081
(C) 0.81
(D) 8.1
(E) 81

CONTINUE ON NEXT PAGE ➡

3. If Papa Smurf can smurf $3s$ smurfs per hour, how many smurfs can he smurf in h hours and m minutes?

(A) $3sh + \dfrac{sm}{20}$

(B) $180sh + 3sm$

(C) $3sm + \dfrac{sh}{20}$

(D) $180sm + 3sh$

(E) $\dfrac{s(h + m)}{20}$

4.

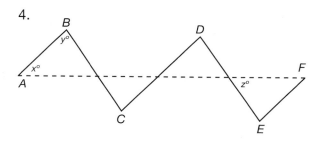

Mel Gibson spouts anti-Semitic ravings as he stumbles along the above path during a straight-line sobriety test.
If $BC \parallel DE$, $x = 50$, and $y = 100$, what is the value of z?
(A) 25
(B) 30
(C) 50
(D) 90
(E) 100

5. Suppose Christina Aguilera's breast surgery scar follows a line in the xy-coordinate plane given by the equation $y = 3x - 8$. If the line crosses the y-axis at the point with coordinates (c, d), what is the value of $c + d$?

(A) −8

(B) $-\dfrac{8}{3}$

(C) 0

(D) $\dfrac{8}{3}$

(E) 8

6.

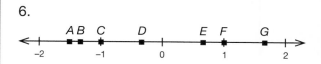

Robert Downey Jr. measures out the above number line with a razor blade. The indicated points have coordinates $A, B, C, D, E, F,$ and G respectively. Which of the following is closest in value to $|A \times E|$?
(A) A
(B) C
(C) E
(D) F
(E) G

CONTINUE ON NEXT PAGE ➡

7. Manny notices that the number of boys who turn their heads as she walks by doubles for every inch she shortens her skirt. If one boy turns his head when Manny wears a 22-inch ankle-length, how many boys will turn their heads if she wears an 11-inch mini?

    (A) 2^9
    (B) 2^{10}
    (C) 2^{11}
    (D) 2^{12}
    (E) 2^{22}

8. Suppose the amount of money (in dollars) one can make from selling x autographs of Lisa Leslie is given by the function $f(x) = \frac{x}{100}$, and the amount of money one can make from selling x autographs of Shaquille O'Neal is given by the function $g(x) = 100x$. How many autographs of Lisa Leslie would one have to sell in order to make $g(10)$ dollars?

    (A) 100
    (B) 1,000
    (C) 10,000
    (D) 100,000
    (E) 1,000,000

CONTINUE ON NEXT PAGE ➡

DIRECTIONS: The remaining questions in this section are grid-in problems. Multiple-choice answers are not provided. Instead, solve the problems directly and enter your answers by filling in the circles of the provided grids.*

Another minute down the drain. Bye-bye, university! Hello, community college! Just answer the grid-in questions already!

9. If Haley Joel Osment's blood alcohol level is 100 percent above the legal limit of 0.08, what is Haley Joel Osment's blood alcohol level?

10. At a Saks Fifth Avenue store, Winona Ryder examines 4 distinct blouses, 5 distinct dresses, and 2 distinct hand-bags. How many different combinations of items can she shoplift if she takes exactly one blouse, two dresses, and a handbag?

11. Five students use up a total of 120 rolls of Charmin to toilet paper their principal's house. If each roll of Charmin contains 352 squares, how many squares of Charmin were used on average (arithmetic mean) by each of the students to TP the principal's house?

12. Jenn's real age, x, and fake ID age, y, satisfy the two equations $y^2 - x^2 = 185$ and $x + y = 37$. What is the value of x?

Actually, we won't force you to fill in the grids, but don't forget that you have to fill in multiple-choice answers and grids on the real SAT exam.

CONTINUE ON NEXT PAGE

13. Gary Coleman needs a loan of k thousand dollars, fast, where $k > 0$ is a solution to the equation $\dfrac{k^2 - 1}{k + 1} = 8$. How much money (in dollars) does Gary Coleman need?

14. Let the total daily cost, in pennies, for children in a small Bangladesh factory to produce x pairs of Nike shoes be given by the function $c(x) = \sqrt{x + 4} + k$, where k is a constant. If 96 pairs of Nike shoes were produced yesterday by children in the small Bangladesh factory for a total cost of 120 cents, what is the value of k?

15. Steven stands exactly 10 feet away from Lauren in order to satisfy Lauren's restraining order against him. Lauren stands exactly 50 feet away from Brian in order to satisfy Brian's restraining order against her. Steven, Lauren, and Brian form a triangle, with each one of them being a vertex of the triangle. If the distance between Steven and Brian is an even integer, what is a possible distance between Steven and Brian?

16. Britney Spears is driven from her home to a rehab clinic at an average speed of 50 mph. When she's informed that there's no drinking allowed at the clinic, Britney immediately turns around and drives back home at an average speed of 80 mph. The total time of her back and forth trip is 2 hours. What is the distance traveled (in miles) between the rehab clinic and Britney's home?

CONTINUE ON NEXT PAGE ➡

17. Timmy falls down a well that is in the shape of a cylinder with a bottom, but open on the top. Lassie barks that the radius of the well is 2 feet and the surface area is 64π feet². How far down (in feet) did Timmy fall?

18.   160, 190, 160, 130, . . .

Suppose Janet Jackson's weight measurements at the beginning of each year are given by the sequence of numbers shown. Each even-numbered term is given by adding $(-1)^{(n-2)/2} \times 30$ to the previous term, and each odd-numbered term, after the first, is given by subtracting $(-1)^{(n+1)/2} \times 30$ from the previous term. What is the 42nd term of the sequence?

S T O P
IF YOU FINISH BEFORE THE TIME ALLOTTED, YOU MAY
CHECK YOUR WORK IN *THIS SECTION ONLY*.

Mathematics Practice Section 3

16 QUESTIONS

TIME: 20 MINUTES

You really just don't have a clue, do you? Stop right here and repeat after me: "Would you like fries with that?" "Can I supersize your order for just ninety-nine cents?" "Please drive forward to the pick-up window to receive your order." Okay, you're good to go.

CONTINUE ON NEXT PAGE ➡

1. The number of times OCD Jake washes his hands during lunch is given by the solution to the equation $3(w - 5) = 18$. What is the value of w?

    (A) $\frac{13}{3}$

    (B) $\frac{23}{3}$

    (C) 11

    (D) 13

    (E) 23

2. Jim's IQ drops 60 percent whenever he sees Tiffany. If Jim's IQ is equal to j when Tiffany is not around, what is Jim's IQ whenever he sees Tiffany?
    (A) $j - 0.006j$
    (B) $j - 0.06j$
    (C) $j - 0.6j$
    (D) $j - 6j$
    (E) $j - 60j$

3.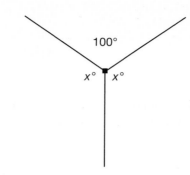

    Before finding her misplaced rubber band, a cutter contemplates cutting herself three times, as shown in the preceding figure. If the three lines all intersect at the same point, what is the value of x?
    (A) 100
    (B) 110
    (C) 120
    (D) 130
    (E) 140

CONTINUE ON NEXT PAGE ➡

4.

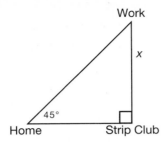

Work

x

45°

Home   Strip Club

Rather than go straight home after work, Alex Rodriguez decides to take the scenic route home by first making a pit stop at the strip club instead. How much longer is the scenic route home than the direct route?

(A) $(2 - \sqrt{2})x$
(B) $(\sqrt{2} - 1)x$
(C) x
(D) $(\sqrt{3} - 1)x$
(E) $(2 - \sqrt{3})x$

5. If the number of freckles on Lindsay Lohan is divisible by both 4 and 38, then it is also divisible by which of the following numbers?

(A) 8
(B) 64
(C) 72
(D) 76
(E) 114

6. If Bryce googled himself x times last month, where x satisfies the equation, $3^{3x} = 81^{x-40}$, what is the value of x?

(A) 160
(B) 200
(C) 240
(D) 320
(E) 400

7. At a Suge Knight party, the ratio of rappers to guns is 2 to 5. The total number of rappers plus guns could be each of the following numbers EXCEPT

(A) 140
(B) 170
(C) 210
(D) 420
(E) 630

CONTINUE ON NEXT PAGE ➡

8. Let a = the average number of funny jokes during an episode of *The Simpsons*; b = the average number of funny jokes during an episode of *Robot Chicken*; c = the average number of funny jokes during an episode of *Cavemen*; and d = the average number of funny jokes during an episode of *How I Met Your Mother*.

   If $abd = 500$ and $abc = 0$, which of the following statements must be true?
   (A) $a < 500$
   (B) $d < 500$
   (C) $b < 250$
   (D) $d = 0$
   (E) $c = 0$

9. In Charlie Sheen's divorce settlement, d is the number of thousand dollars paid out, y is the number of years of marriage, and e is the number of documented extramarital affairs Charlie is caught having during the term of the marriage. If the divorce settlement can be written as $\frac{d}{5} - 20e = 2 - 2y$, what is d in terms of y and e?
   (A) $d = 10e - 1y + 1$
   (B) $d = 100e - 10y + 10$
   (C) $d = 10 - 10y - 100e$
   (D) $d = 20e - 10y + 10$
   (E) $d = 100e - 2y + 2$

10. Peter's dad rips Peter a new hole with radius π and circumference r. What is the area of Peter's new hole?
    (A) πr^2
    (B) $2\pi r$
    (C) π
    (D) π^3
    (E) r

11. A rock star is a baby daddy to three children with three different groupies on three different continents. The children's ages are given by consecutive even integers, and the sum of the three ages is 30. What is the age of the oldest child?
    (A) 8
    (B) 9
    (C) 10
    (D) 11
    (E) 12

CONTINUE ON NEXT PAGE ➡

12.

GAYNESS LEVEL

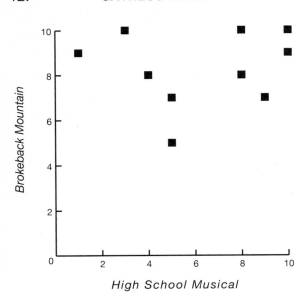

Ten students are asked to rank the level of "gayness" (on a scale of 0 to 10) of *High School Musical* and *Brokeback Mountain*. The results are given in the scatterplot shown. If *x* equals the median gayness level ranking given to *High School Musical* and *y* equals the average (arithmetic mean) gayness level ranking given to *Brokeback Mountain*, what is the value of $x - y$?

(A) −4.3
(B) −1.8
(C) 0
(D) 1.8
(E) 4.3

13. If some people who like Darth Vader also like Jabba the Hutt, some people who like Jabba the Hutt also like Boba Fett, and nobody at all likes Jar Jar Binks, which of the following must also be true?

(A) Some people who like Darth Vader also like Boba Fett.
(B) Some people who like Boba Fett also like Darth Vader.
(C) More people like Jabba the Hutt than like Boba Fett.
(D) No person who likes both Darth Vader and Jabba the Hutt also likes Jar Jar Binks.
(E) No person who likes both Darth Vader and Boba Fett also likes Jabba the Hutt.

CONTINUE ON NEXT PAGE ➡

14.   COLLEGE STUDENT FOOD GROUP

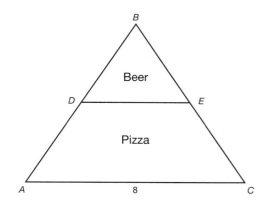

If $\overline{DE} \parallel \overline{AC}$, $AC = 8$, and $DE = 4$, what is the value of $\frac{BD}{DA}$?

(A) $\frac{\sqrt{2}}{2}$

(B) $\frac{1}{2}$

(C) 1

(D) $\sqrt{2}$

(E) 2

15. Each day Norbert is stuffed into a locker that measures 6 feet high, 1 foot wide, and 1.5 feet deep. The school replaces its lockers with new ones that measure 10 percent smaller in each of the three dimensions. How much smaller in volume are the new lockers that Norbert is stuffed inside?

(A) 0.009 feet^3

(B) 0.810 feet^3

(C) 0.900 feet^3

(D) 2.439 feet^3

(E) 24.39 feet^3

CONTINUE ON NEXT PAGE ➡

16.

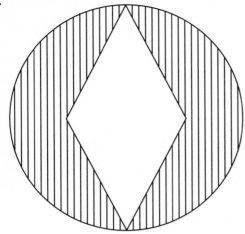

After a night of heavy drinking, Michelle wakes up with no memory of the night before and with a tattoo on her butt in the shape of the figure shown. The diameter of the circle is 6 and the quadrilateral has all four sides of equal length. As well, the shorter diagonal of the quadrilateral passes through the center of the circle and has a length of 3. What is the area of the shaded region of the figure?

(A) $9\pi - \frac{3}{4}$

(B) $9\pi - 9$

(C) $9\pi - 18$

(D) $36\pi - 9$

(E) $36\pi - 18$

S T O P

IF YOU FINISH BEFORE THE TIME ALLOTTED, YOU MAY
CHECK YOUR WORK IN *THIS SECTION ONLY*.

PART 7
ANSWERS

Answer Key

CRITICAL READING

PRACTICE SECTION 1

1. C	2. C	3. D	4. D	5. B	6. E
7. B	8. C	9. A	10. C	11. D	12. C
13. B	14. A	15. B	16. E	17. B	18. C
19. C	20. A	21. D	22. D	23. E	24. D

PRACTICE SECTION 2

1. B	2. B	3. E	4. D	5. E	6. A
7. E	8. A	9. C	10. D	11. E	12. A
13. C	14. C	15. A	16. D	17. C	18. E
19. B	20. D	21. E	22. E	23. A	24. A

PRACTICE SECTION 3

1. E	2. A	3. B	4. C	5. D	6. C
7. C	8. C	9. A	10. D	11. B	12. E
13. A	14. D	15. D	16. C	17. D	18. B
19. E					

WRITING

PRACTICE SECTION 1

1. E	2. D	3. A	4. D	5. C	6. E
7. D	8. B	9. C	10. C	11. E	12. B
13. B	14. A	15. D	16. D	17. C	18. D
19. D	20. B	21. B	22. C	23. E	24. E
25. A	26. D	27. B	28. E	29. C	30. B
31. C	32. E	33. E	34. D	35. B	

PRACTICE SECTION 2

1. D	2. E	3. C	4. E	5. B	6. A
7. D	8. B	9. C	10. B	11. C	12. D
13. B	14. A				

MATHEMATICS

PRACTICE SECTION 1

1. D	2. D	3. E	4. B	5. B	6. C
7. C	8. C	9. D	10. C	11. E	12. D
13. A	14. E	15. C	16. C	17. E	18. D
19. E	20. C				

PRACTICE SECTION 2

1. B	2. C	3. A	4. B	5. A	6. D
7. C	8. D	9. .16	10. 80	11. 8448	12. 16
13. 9000	14. 110	15. 42, 44, 46, 48, 50, 52, 54, 56, or 58			
16. 61.5	17. 15	18. 190			

PRACTICE SECTION 3

1. C	2. C	3. D	4. A	5. D	6. A
7. B	8. E	9. B	10. D	11. E	12. B
13. D	14. C	15. D	16. B		

Scoring

$$\text{Raw Score} = \text{Number Correct} - \frac{\text{Number Incorrect}}{4}$$

(Round fractions to the nearest whole number.)

TABLE 1: CRITICAL READING

RAW SCORE	RESULT
67	Awesome! Great job, Four-Eyes!
59–66	The good news—you did really great. The bad news—the way things are headed, you may have to learn Chinese instead.
38–58	Congratulations! You're in debt!
24–37	Don't feel bad. Community college is still a college.
21–23	Who needs books when you've got TV?
18–20	Let's clean toilets!
14–17	Tarzan not do so good.
10–13	Does it matter? You can't read this anyway.
1–9	You're special!
−16–0	*No habla inglés.*
−17	You clearly hate your parents, as you obviously know the answers and got them all wrong on purpose.

TABLE 2: WRITING*

RAW SCORE	RESULT
49	Awesome! Great job, Shakespeare!
41–48	The good news—you did really great. The bad news—"English degree" and "high-paying job" are seldom found in the same sentence.
26–40	Congratulations! You're in debt!
17–25	Don't feel bad. Community college is still a college.
11–16	Let's clean toilets!
7–10	Tarzan not do so good.
1–6	You're special!
–11–0	*No habla inglés.*
–12	You clearly hate your parents, as you obviously know the answers and got them all wrong on purpose.

TABLE 3: MATH

RAW SCORE	RESULT
54	Awesome! You're an honorary Asian!
48–53	The good news—you did really great. The bad news—you're still a virgin.
31–47	Congratulations! You're in debt!
21–30	Don't feel bad. Community college is still a college.
16–20	You can always drink Tang and *pretend* you're an astronaut.
10–15	Let's clean toilets!
1–9	You don't even know how to calculate your raw score, do you?
–10–0	You're special!
–11	You clearly hate your parents, as you obviously know the answers and got them all wrong on purpose.

Note: Don't forget—on the actual SAT exam, there is also an essay.

Solutions to Selected Problems

CRITICAL READING PRACTICE SECTION 1

2. One may question the beliefs or motivation of the test *makers*, but not the test itself. *Efficacy* means *usefulness*, and it is quite appropriate to question the usefulness of the test.

3. Investigators, who do their job properly, painstakingly examine all the evidence and then come to a conclusion based on the facts. They don't *realize* or *prognosticate* (which means *predict* or *prophecy*) or *charge* (which means *accuse*), and they don't perform *cursory* (which means *superficial*) investigations.

5. If you just found out your left boob popped out of your dress and everyone was taking pictures of your boob job gone wrong, how would you feel? Not very good, I imagine. The only answer choices that fit both blanks are (A) and (B), but (B) is the stronger choice because Tara would not just be surprised, she would feel *terribly ashamed*, which is *mortified*.

6. The examples in the passage are ones that use animation to suggest that a product really works. Of the answer choices, only (E) is comparable. Answer choices (A) through (D) involve animation only in the form of a cartoon spokesperson or character.

8. The passage does not mention a policy decision or a scientific approach, and it doesn't defend a health study either, so we can eliminate (A), (B), and (D). Although an authority is quoted in the passage, that is not the primary purpose of the passage.

11. Zorlak is the imaginary name the author gives to the presumed head of the alien invasion. While both (B) and (D) are accurate statements, (D) is more accurate than (B).

14. Choice (B) is too broad. The author thinks *some* scientists are left-wing radicals, not all. Choice (C) is similarly too broad—the author believes some science is good. There is no support for (D) or (E). However, (A) is supported. The author talks about extraterrestrials as though they were a certainty.

15. The author's primary purpose is to advocate a policy concerning the question of Iran and nuclear weapons. One could argue that other answer choices are true statements as well, to varying degrees, but they are not the primary purpose of the passage.

16. Entomology is the study of insects, so we can eliminate (A). The author addresses the general public directly, so we can eliminate (C) and (D) as well. The author also provides an opinion rather than a review.

20. The phrase, "there are upsides too," supports answer choice (A).

22. The author argues that just like M.A.D. broke Russia economically in the Cold War, so too would M.A.D. break Iran economically.

24. For the policy of M.A.D. to cause the financial collapse of Iran, as the author argues, neither side of the conflict would actually use their nuclear weapons. If Iran is currently ruled by radical Mullahs operating on extreme religious principals rather than logic, the argument falls apart.

CRITICAL READING PRACTICE SECTION 2

1. Fran wants a divorce because she caught her husband doing something to his secretary that he really shouldn't have been doing. *Ruthless* is the best fit. Fran wants to get back at her husband and make him rue the day he was born.

4. Barbarians are known to pillage.

5. The "gazpacho tasted like deer piss" comment, together with the parallel structure of the sentence, suggests that both of the blanks should be negative comments as well. Answer choice (E) is the only answer choice that provides truly negative comments for both blanks.

6. *Conjecture* means *a statement made without proof. Amity* means *friendship. Nuance* means *subtle variation. Demagoguery* means *appealing to popular prejudices for political gain. Gesticulation* means *signaling.*

9. We can eliminate (A) because the passage doesn't even mention consolation prizes. In addition, while (B), (D), and (E) may be true, they are not the given reason why every contestant is a winner. The reason can be found in phrases such as "expand their horizons," "promote their personal growth," and "benefits from the experience."

10. We can eliminate (B) because the passage doesn't even mention interest rates. Although (A), (C), and (E) are all mentioned, and even in relation to the economy, none of these answers are as accurate as (D). The passage, as a whole, describes how large parts of the economy depend on traditional roles for geeks and beauties.

12. Let's examine each answer choice:
(A) Passage 1 is concerned with personal growth and public good, while Passage 2 is concerned with economics regardless of how individuals are treated.
(B) The first part of the statement is true, but we can't be certain about the second part. We don't know from Passage 2 if the author watches the show or not.
(C) From Passage 1, it seems as if the author wants *positive* social experimentation, not social experimentation for its own sake.
(D) and (E) These statements may or may not be true, but aren't supported well enough in the passages.

13. The general tone of the passage seems to be one of genuine interest in the idea of being a billionaire. The author does not describe anger concerning wealth disparity, so we can eliminate (A). The main point of the passage is not about the author's private life, so we can eliminate (B). The author is

not a billionaire and does not relate to the *Forbes* list personally, so we can eliminate (D). Finally, the author seems captivated by the notion of being a billionaire, not simply by the fact that the number of billionaires is growing, so we can eliminate (E).

17. The portion describes how the author thinks people can convince themselves that they need more and more money, no matter how much money they make. The portion does not describe an example of mind over matter. If anything, matter is affecting the mind. The portion does not describe financial markets. The portion is not a case study, and does not describe an increasing cultural phenomenon either. The portion does not describe a physical principle. The portion does describe how the author suspects people's psychology changes over time as they make more money.

18. The second paragraph describes how the number billion is a truly large number, and the fourth paragraph describes how the number is so large, most people wouldn't even know how to spend that amount of money. In both cases, the common point is that for most average people, a billion dollars is so big that they really don't comprehend it. The points in (B) and (C) are not made in the second paragraph and the point in (D) is not made in the fourth paragraph. Aspects of the author's private life are described in both paragraphs, but his private life is not the point of either paragraph.

21. The portion in question describes scrounging around in a onesy sofa and finding a quarter. The irony refers to searching for change when the furniture itself is made of money. Choice (A) is not ironic. No mention is made to feeling uncomfortable, so we can eliminate (B). Similarly, no mention is made to an Alanis Morissette song, so we can eliminate (C). Answer choice (D) could be a true statement involving a case of irony, but it isn't the specific irony mentioned in the passage.

23. The author makes no mention of billionaires causing much strife in the world, so we can eliminate (B). Similarly, the author does not discuss billionaires inheriting their wealth, so we can eliminate (C). Both (D) and (E) are discussed in the passage, but as imaginations of the author. The author does not believe either of those statements in real life. However, the author clearly believes that billionaires are human beings with human foibles such as pettiness and greed.

CRITICAL READING PRACTICE SECTION 3

3.   The word "but" tells us that Tony felt one way at first and then felt very differently, so the two blanks should convey distinct emotions. This eliminates (C). In addition, the fact that the call was "simply meant as a distraction" suggests that the second blank should convey a negative emotion. This eliminates (A), (D), and (E).

5.   *Prosaic* means *dull* or *ordinary*, and Triple-Crown winners are neither dull nor ordinary, so we can eliminate (A) based on the first blank. The use of the word "famous" also suggests that the first blank should mean "famous" as well, so this eliminates (C). We can next eliminate (E) based on the second blank, because a horse would not be able to live on in other horses it smote. So we're down to (B) and (D), which both sound okay at first. However, horses aren't usually said to inspire other horses, while they are said to sire other horses (*sired* means *fathered*).

7.   Passage 2 refers to specific phrases in Passage 1, so from Passage 2 we can infer that Passage 1 was in fact an e-mail sent by the author of Passage 1 to the author of Passage 2 and Passage 2 was her e-mail response back. More specifically, this e-mail was an unwelcome request for a prom date. Therefore, (C) is the correct choice instead of (D).

9.   "Surely, she is Venus personified"—I is correct. "Her eyes, like two precious sapphires, sparkle dazzlingly in the moonlight."—The woman's eyes are compared to sapphires, not to the moonlight itself. II is incorrect. "Her creamy hide glistens softly in the morning dew"—The woman's skin is described as creamy. The woman is not compared to the morning dew itself. III is incorrect.

10.   "Her eyes, like two precious sapphires"—eyes. "Her smile, a glimmering beacon of pearls"—teeth. "her mountains heaving with every step"—breasts "Her creamy hide glistens softly"—skin. There are no references to her arms.

12.   "She" is *compared to* both Helen of Troy and the goddess of love, but "She" does not actually refer to either of them.

14.   The paragraph in question talks about the suitor's writing. The author does not refer to the suitor's weight or discuss anything about fine cheeses. As well, while the author calls the suitor both a stalker and a Troll doll with zits, she is not referring to those statements in this paragraph, which is about his writing.

15.   No mention is ever made concerning the suitor being poor or not saying "please," so we can safely eliminate (C) and (E).
(A)   One of the stated reasons the suitor was rejected is that he plays the tuba. However, was he rejected because a tuba is a musical instrument, or because a tuba is a tuba? If he played an electric guitar, she most likely would not have a problem with it.
(B)   One of the stated reasons the suitor was rejected is that his feet stink. She thinks it could very well be a medical condition, but she isn't rejecting him because of a possible medical condition. If he possibly had a cold, but his feet didn't stink, she most likely would not have a problem with it.
(D)   One of the stated reasons the suitor was rejected is that he's not physically attractive. In other words, his physical exterior is lacking.

16. The answer can be found in the third paragraph of Passage 2. The author is turned off by the suitor's "cheeseball" way of asking her out on a date, and by his references to female body parts and sex. While all the other suggestions given in the other answer choices are probably a very good idea as well, they were not included in the specific advice given by the author.

18. Given the extremely negative tone used throughout Passage 2, we can safely eliminate (A) and (C). The author of Passage 2 also never threatens any bodily harm to the author of Passage 1, so we can eliminate (D) as well. We're now left with (B) and (E). While we may be tempted to choose (E) because the author of Passage 2 states "leave me alone" numerous times, that would be an incorrect choice. The author only wrote Passage 2 because the author of Passage 1 wouldn't leave her alone. She would much rather just not have any dealings with him. Therefore, she would most likely try to avoid him if she could.

19.

(A) The author of Passage 2 believes "He" is stalking "She," but the author of Passage 1 believes "He" is just being persistent.

(B) The author of Passage 1 clearly believes "She" is worthy of being compared to precious gemstones, but we have no indication of how the author of Passage 2 feels.

(C) The question was answered, albeit in the negative.

(D) Neither author believes "She" is an imaginary person.

(E) Both authors seem to agree with this statement.

From Passage 1: "No, he must not think them, let alone speak such lofty dreams as these."

From Passage 2: "Wake up and smell the reality, you dweeb."

WRITING PRACTICE SECTION 1

1. Too Wordy

The Internet turned 38 years old this year, and it is still a virgin, living at home with its parents.

2. Modifier Comparison Error

Of all the Flavor Flav girls, she was definitely the most skanky.

3. This sentence is actually correct as written.

Choices (B) and (C) create a comma splice, and (D) and (E) incorrectly have a conjunction after a semicolon.

4. Shifting Verb Tenses

The tricky part, though, is that you need to know that "went" is the past tense of "to go," while "gone" is the past participle of "to go."

At the United Nations Global Summit on Young People, 180 nations pledged to make the world a better place for kids, and then went back to killing each other.

5. Ambiguous and Too Wordy

The sentence is ambiguous (who is "they"?) and too wordy. Only (C) is neither ambiguous nor wordy.

In space, no one can hear you fart.

6. Mixing Up Singular and Plural

There is one skirt, so the pronoun should be "it" instead of "them." This sentence is difficult because the pronouns come before the skirt is mentioned.

Maya purchased it because she thought it was pretty, but she had no idea that the skirt made her butt look like two Great Danes fighting over a milk bone.

7. Shifting Verb Tenses (and Lack of Parallelism)

It should be "shutting" and "remaining."

I like to celebrate Halloween each year by shutting off all the lights and remaining very quiet.

8. Sentence Fragment

Answer choice (C) still leaves a sentence fragment, while (D) and (E) use the conjunction "and," which doesn't match up as well with the word "may" and loses the relationship between the first and second half of the sentence.

Jesus may love you, but I just want to be friends.

9. Comma Splice—Subordinate Clause

A semicolon should be used instead of the comma, as in (C). Answer choice (B) also has a semicolon, but (B) incorrectly adds the conjunction "as" after the semicolon. Choice (D) fixes the comma splice, but loses the relationship between the two parts of the sentence, as if the two parts of the sentence were not related. Choice (E) also fixes the comma splice, but it rearranges the sentence in a way that is slightly ambiguous, suggesting that if I did not think you were Antoine, I would not be apologizing.

I truly apologize for squeezing your ass during the huddle; I totally thought you were Antoine.

10. Too Wordy

The popular Internet teen social networking site has over 80 million members, including thousands upon thousands of registered sex offenders.

11. Dangling Participle

The undercover police officer didn't claim innocence—Barney the Dinosaur did. Answer choice (B) has the same problem. While (C) and (D) both make it clear that Barney the Dinosaur is the one claiming his innocence, neither (C) nor (D) are as clearly phrased as (E).

Although he claimed his rendition of "I Love You, You Love Me" was completely innocent, Barney the Dinosaur was arrested last night for propositioning the undercover police officer.

12. Shifting Verb Tenses

Although he never lost a single game of Twister, Mr. Fantastic was quite often accused of cheating.

13. Shifting Pronouns

To correspond with "athlete," "he" or "she" should be used instead of "one."

I believe that once an athlete thanks Jesus for a win, she should be immediately disqualified for using a performance enhancer.

14. Improper Pronoun Case

Teenage Casper desperately wished that he and Wendy could be more than just friends.

15. Logical Comparison Error

Mary-Kate lost much more weight than Ashley, not "Ashley's diet."

Mary-Kate and Ashley went on the exact same diet, but somehow Mary-Kate lost much more weight than Ashley.

16. Mixing Up Singular and Plural

There was one sighting, so the verb "were" should have been "was" instead.

The paranormal detective was in particularly high spirits until he discovered that his Sasquatch sighting was in fact just a case of Robin Williams out on a camping trip.

17. Lack of Parallelism

If "get all dressed up" is the first thing people do, then the other things they do should also be written in a parallel way.

On a national day of prayer, people get all dressed up, take their families to church, and pray that their kids don't get hit on by a priest.

18. Logical Comparison Error

Hannah received more presents than Julie, not "Julie's divorce."

Hannah's parents and Julie's parents both split up around the same time, but Hannah, due to a bitter custody battle, received way more presents than Julie.

19. Shifting Verb Tenses

"Pulls out" should be "pulled out" instead.

Yugi realized something was amiss with his playing deck when, instead of drawing the Dark Magician, he pulled out a seven of diamonds.

20. Mixing Up Singular and Plural

There are three side effects—plural.

The most common side effects include nausea, diarrhea, and sudden death.

21. Idiom Error

We don't say "help to wonder"—we say "help but wonder."

One cannot help but wonder if Bill Gates tells his old classmates to "suck it" every time he peruses his high school yearbook.

22. Mixing Up Singular and Plural

There are multiple coins and they "come in" three different varieties.

The limited-edition commemorative Jamaican coins, featuring the likeness of late reggae star Bob Marley, come in three different varieties—gold, silver, and ganja.

25. Mixing Up Adjectives and Adverbs

Britney solemnly vowed that from now on she will do her laundry before she goes out clubbing.

26. Shifting Pronouns

If "you" hurry to your local video store, "you" can still see the movie.

Scientists have discovered that pollutants from as far away as Asia have been crossing oceans, reaching all the way to the East Coast, and, in a related story, if you hurry to your local video store, you can still catch *Around the World in Eighty Days,* starring Jackie Chan.

27. Mixing Up Words — Diction Error

The ghost wanted the ghost whisperer to "speak up" rather than "speak out."

The disconcerted apparition asked the ghost whisperer to speak up, as he could not hear a single word she was saying.

29. Ambiguous

The sentence states that Paula did not comment on *William's pitch*, not William himself, so Simon's comment of "grating and offensive" should refer to William's pitch, not William himself.

Paula did not have the heart to comment on William's pitch, but Simon called it grating and offensive, and proclaimed that the only way William would ever make money through singing is if people paid him to stop.

30. The sentence currently is missing a conjunction just before "you must have bought at the dollar store." We can therefore eliminate (A), and also (C), (D), and (E), which don't serve to fix the problem.

32. The sentence begins a new paragraph and is slightly vague in regards to its pronouns. The "She" and "she" in question both refer to Mom, but replacing "She" at the beginning of the sentence makes the sentence much clearer.

35. We can eliminate (C) because the author clearly does not forgive Grandma, and we can eliminate (E) because the note makes it clear that the author will not miss Grandma. Although (A) and (D) both fit the tone of the note, they are not as effective as (B) as a concluding sentence. An effective concluding sentence would relate back to the beginning and tie the entire note together. The first sentence describes how Mom is forcing the author to write the note, so (B) effectively concludes the note by saying that the author thinks Mom's directive has now been fulfilled and the author can stop now.

WRITING PRACTICE SECTION 2

1. Shifting Pronouns

The pronoun for *Ozzy* is *he*, not *one*, so we can eliminate (A), (C), and (E). Choice (B) has the correct pronoun, but the incorrect verb tense, *needs*.

Ozzy first tried to pee the fire out, but finally realized he needed to call the fire department.

2. Mixing Up Singular and Plural

There are two girls — plural. They want to become models — not a model.

Tiffany and Khandi became anorexic soon after they decided to become models.

3. Dangling Participle

The video store didn't find the grocery store out of turkey — *I* did. Answer choice (E) has a similar problem. Choice (B) lacks a noun after the participial phrase. Choice (D) is ambiguous and makes it sound like I found out there was no turkey at the grocery store while I as at the video store.

Finding the grocery store fresh out of turkey on Thanksgiving Day, I went to the video store and rented the latest Rob Schneider movie instead.

4. Too Wordy and Ambiguous

    The word "Internet" is believed to have come from the Latin words "Inter" and "Net," which mean "Star Trek" and "porn."

5. Sentence Fragment

    The other answer choices all fix the problem, but (C) contains the extra word *but* (which is unnecessary because it follows the word *except*), and (D) and (E) are too wordy.

    Disneyland in Hong Kong is much like Disneyland here, except each night after the Main Street Parade all the cartoon animals are eaten.

7. Mixing Up Words — Diction Error

    The words may be are mixed up with maybe.

    A top U.S. commander said that Osama bin Laden may be hiding in eastern Afghanistan, or possibly western Afghanistan, or Pakistan, or maybe Yemen, or even somewhere else entirely.

8. Passive Verb

    Researchers say that teenagers who are vegetarians are much healthier than other teens; that is, they're healthier until the other teens beat them up for being different.

9. Passive Verb

    Answer choice (D) doesn't fix the problem, and (B) and (E) are confusing (the money is going toward singing lessons, not vice versa).

    Hilary Duff announced that a portion of all ticket sales from her upcoming concert tour will go toward charity, while the rest of the money will go toward singing lessons.

10. Mixing Up Words — Diction Error

    The error in this sentence involves mixing up the words *except* and *accept*.

    Scientists say that greenhouse gases are causing the Earth to heat up even faster than predicted, but luckily there is no cause for alarm because the fossil fuel industry refuses to accept the existence of global warming.

11. Modifier Comparison Error

    In a comparison with "all" losers, the proper modifier is "biggest," not "bigger."

    Gerald felt like the biggest loser of all when even MySpace Tom rejected his friendship.

12. Comma Splice — Coordinating Conjunction

    Answer choice (B) is incorrect because the word "but" captures an incorrect relationship between the two parts of the sentence. Choice (C) is missing a conjunction (as it follows a comma). Choice (E) is still a comma splice.

    Hulk Hogan was inducted into the World Wrestling Entertainment Hall of Fame, thus confirming his place as one of the all-time great fake sportsmen.

13. Comma Splice

    Choice (C) incorrectly has a conjunction after a semicolon. Choice (D) contains an incorrect verb tense. Choice (E) contains an ambiguous pronoun.

    Courtney declared she would remain faithful to her virginity pledge, but Dylan convinced her that prom night was an allowable exception.

14. This sentence is actually correct as written.

    The pronoun in (B) is vague. Choice (C) is also vague (because at least one of the extramarital offspring is his). Choice (D) mixes up singular and plural. Choice (E) is a sentence fragment.

MATHEMATICS PRACTICE SECTION 1

1. Using a shorthand notation:
20 pounds = 12 minutes, so
1 pound = 12/20 minutes = 3/5 minutes.
Therefore, 30 pounds = 30 (3/5) minutes = 18 minutes.

4. The only element common to both sets is Lance. Therefore, I Heart Brad $\cap$ I Heart Denzel = {Lance}.

6. 500 ahead + 1 Steven + 500 behind = 1,001 people.

7. $x = y + 5,000$, so $x > y$. Therefore, Frankie owes: $5x - 5y = 5(x - y) = 5(5,000) = 25,000$.

8. Construct a right triangle with the hypotenuse being the distance, d, between Tristan and his starting point, and with the other two sides having lengths of 8 miles and 6 miles respectively. Apply the Pythagorean Theorem to get $d^2 = 8^2 + 6^2 = 100$. Therefore, $d = 10$.

9. The love triangle is isosceles, so the two angles opposite the two equal length sides are equal. The total of all the angles in the bisected triangle also add up to 180, so $x + 55 + 90 = 180$. Therefore, $x = 35$.

11. Let s equal the sum of the scores of the other 49 students and let w equal Wong-Li's score. Then, $s/49 = 10$, which means $s = 490$. In addition, (sum of 50 scores)/50 = 12. But the sum of the 50 scores = $s + w$. Therefore, $(s + w)/50 = 12$, which means $w = (50)(12) - s = 600 - 490 = 110$.

13. If all 5 African-American men look exactly alike to the Caucasian, then each of the 5 men have an equal 1 in 5 chance of being chosen.

16. Let A = the current age of Ashton Kutcher. Let B = the current age of Demi Moore. Then,

$$A + B = 76 \qquad (1), \text{ and}$$
$$A - 14 = (B - 14) / 2 \quad \text{ or}$$
$$2A - B = 14 \qquad (2)$$

Add (1) and (2) to get $3A = 90$. Therefore, $A = 30$. In twenty years, Ashton Kutcher will be $30 + 20 = 50$.

17. Original Volume = s^3.
New Volume = $(3s)^3 = 27s^3$.
Therefore, New Volume : Original Volume = $27s^3 : s^3$ = 27:1 = 27s:s.

18. The variable h is between 8 and 12 inches taller than Prissy, which means h is 10 inches taller than Prissy plus or minus 2. In other words, h is 74 plus or minus 2.

19. The equation for Kyle's line is $y = mx + b$. The line is perpendicular to Haley's line, so $m = -1/3$. In addition, it passes through the point (3,11) where the two lines intersect. Therefore, $11 = (-1/3)(3) + b$. Therefore, $b = 12$.

20. Plug into the definition to get $(a - 2)^2 - 2(a - 2) = a^2 - 2a$. Expand the terms to get $a^2 - 4a + 4 - 2a + 4 = a^2 - 2a$. The a^2 terms cancel each other out, so we get $4a = 8$. Therefore, $a = 2$.

MATHEMATICS PRACTICE SECTION 2

1. Twenty packs of Trojans cost $120, so 1 pack of Trojans costs $6. Therefore, beaker:pack of Trojans = 4:6 = 2:3.

4.

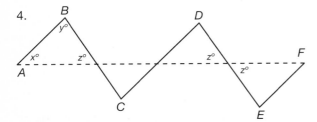

The variable z equals its vertical angle. This vertical angle equals the third angle in the triangle with x and y because AF intersects the two parallel lines BC and DE. Therefore, $x + y + z = 180$, which means $z = 180 - x - y = 180 - 50 - 100 = 30$.

5. The line crosses the y-axis when $x = 0$. Therefore $c = 0$ and $d = 3(0) - 8 = -8$. Therefore, $c + d = 0 + (-8) = -8$.

6. We can approximate point A as $-3/2$ and point E as $2/3$. Therefore $|A \times E|$ is approximately equal to $|(-3/2)(2/3)| = |-1| = 1$, which is point F.

8. Plug 10 into g to get $g(10) = 10^3 = 1,000$. Therefore, $f(x) = 1,000$, which means $x/100 = 1,000$, or $x = 100,000$.

10. The total number of combinations is given by multiplying the number of combinations for each item.

The number of ways to choose 1 blouse out of 4 is 4.

The number of ways to choose 2 dresses out of 5 is $(5 \times 4) / 2 = 10$.

The number of ways to choose 1 handbag out of 2 is 2.

Therefore the number of different combinations of items Winona Ryder can shoplift is $4 \times 10 \times 2 = 80$.

11. Total squares = 120 rolls $\times$ 352 squares per roll = 42,240 squares. The average for each student = Total/5 = 8,448 squares (which is filled in as 8448).

13. $(k^2 - 1)/(k + 1) = (k + 1)(k - 1)/(k + 1) = k - 1$. Therefore $k - 1 = 8$, or $k = 9$. Remember, though, that k represents the number of thousands of dollars Gary Coleman needs. The correct answer is 9,000 (which is filled in as 9000). Thank you, Cash-Call!

14. $120 = \sqrt{96 + 4} + k = 10 + k$, so $110 = k$.

15. Let d be the distance between Steven and Brian. From the Triangle Inequality, we have $50 - 10 < d < 50 + 10$, or $40 < d < 60$. We are told that d is an even integer, so the possible correct answers are 42, 44, 46, 48, 50, 52, 54, 56, and 58.

16. Distance = Rate $\times$ Time

She travels the same distance either way, so $(50)(t_1) = (80)(t_2)$.

We also know that the total time is 2 hours, so $t_1 + t_2 = 2$.

Substitute one equation into the other to get, $t_1 + (5/8)(t_1) = 2$, which means $t_1 = 2(8/13) = 16/13$.

Finally, plug this back into the distance equation to get $d = (50)(t_1) = (50)(16/13) = 61.5$ miles (when rounded).

17. The surface area of a closed cylinder is given by the equation $2\pi Rh + 2\pi R^2$. Because the well is in the shape of a cylinder minus the top, we need to subtract the area of the top, which is πR^2. Therefore, the surface area of the well is given by the equation SA of Well $= 2\pi Rh + \pi R^2$.

But Lassie tells us that the surface area is 64π and that the radius $R = 2$. Therefore, $2\pi Rh + \pi R^2 = 64\pi$, which means $2\pi(2)h + \pi(2)^2 = 64\pi$, or $4h + 4 = 64$. Therefore, $h = 15$.

That's one smart dog! Although, why didn't she just tell us the height directly, instead of making us waste all this time figuring it out? Bitch.

MATHEMATICS PRACTICE SECTION 3

2.   Jim's IQ starts at j and drops 60 percent, so whenever he sees Tiffany, his IQ is given by $j - (60/100)j$, which is the same as $j - 0.6j$.

3.   The total degree amount is 360. Therefore, $x + x + 100 = 360$, which means $2x = 260$, so $x = 130$.

5. If a number is divisible by both 4 and 38, then it is also divisible by the least common multiple of 4 and 38. $4 = 2 \times 2$ and $38 = 2 \times 19$. The least common multiple of 4 and 38 is therefore $2 \times 2 \times 19 = 76$.

7.   If we know rappers/guns = 2/5, then the number of rappers = $2k$ and the number of guns = $5k$ for some positive integer k. The total can thus be written as:
Total = rappers + guns = $2k + 5k = 7k$.
The total must therefore be a multiple of 7.

8.   If $abc = 0$ then at least one of a, b, or c equals zero. If $abd = 500$ then neither a, nor b, nor d can equal zero. Therefore $c = 0$. Great work, ABC!

10.   Area of Hole = $\pi(\text{radius})^2 = \pi(\pi)^2 = \pi^3$.

12. *High School Musical* rankings: 1 3 4 5 5 8 8 9 10 10
Brokeback Mountain rankings: 5 7 7 8 8 9 9 10 10 10
$x = (5 + 8)/2 = 6.5$.
$y = (5 + 7 + 7 + 8 + 8 + 9 + 9 + 10 + 10 + 10)/10 = 8.3$.
Therefore, $x - y = -1.8$.

18. The pattern repeats as 160, 190, 160, 130, 160, 190, 160, 130, ..., going up and down and up and down like a yo-yo every 4 years. If you divide 42 by 4, the remainder is 2, which means that the 42nd term of the sequence is the same as the 2nd term of the sequence.

13. Nobody at all likes Jar Jar Binks, so that includes a person who likes both Darth Vader and Jabba the Hutt.

14. Because the two line segments are parallel, it means $\angle BAC = \angle BDE$ and $\angle BCA = \angle BED$. The two triangles BAC and BDE therefore have all three equivalent angles, which means the two triangles are similar. Therefore, because the ratio of AC to DE is 2, the ratio of BA to BD is also 2. This means that BD is half the length of BA and DA is also half the length of BA. Therefore, $BD/DA = 1$.

15. Old Volume = $(6)(1)(1.5) = 9$ feet^3.
The dimensions of the smaller lockers are:
Height = $(0.9)(6) = 5.4$, Width = $(0.9)(1) = 0.9$, and Depth = $(0.9)(1.5) = 1.35$. Therefore,
New Volume = $(5.4)(0.9)(1.35) = 6.561$ feet^3.
Difference in Volume = $(9 - 6.561)$ feet$^3 = 2.439$ feet^3.

16. Shaded Area = Area of Circle − Area of Quadrilateral.

For the quadrilateral, divide it by the shorter diagonal into two triangles. The base of the two triangles is the shorter diagonal and the height of both triangles is the radius of the circle. Therefore, Area of Quadrilateral = $2((1/2)(b)(h)) = 2((1/2)(3)(3)) = 9$.

Therefore, Shaded Area = $\pi r^2 - 9 = 9\pi - 9$.

Appendix

SOME COMMON DICTION ERRORS

- accept – except
- adverse – averse
- affect – effect
- all ready – already
- allude – elude
- allusion – illusion
- any one – anyone
- breath – breathe
- capital – capitol
- complement – compliment
- confidant – confident
- could of (not proper English) – could have
- desert – dessert
- eminent – imminent
- farther – further
- it's – its
- lay – lie
- peace – piece
- principal – principle
- than – then
- their – there – they're
- wander – wonder
- who's – whose
- you're – your

SOME COMMON IDIOMS

- act as
- associate with
- based on
- capable of
- choose to
- comply with
- concerned with
- conform to
- conscious of
- consistent with
- different from
- equivalent to
- except for
- identical to
- in contrast to
- indicate that
- listen to
- opposed to
- preoccupied with
- refer to
- regard as
- responsible for
- unique to